NINJA FOODI SMARTLID COOKBOOK FOR BEGINNERS

1600 Days of Easy, Flavorful and Innovative Air Fry, Pressure Cook, Slow Cook, and More Recipes Enhancing Your Ninja Foodi Experience with 4-Week Meal Plan

Kent Collins

TABLE OF
CONTENT

INTRODUCTION   **01**

CHAPTER 1: NINJA FOODI SMART XL PRESSURE COOKER   **02**

CHAPTER 2: BREAKFAST   **08**

CHAPTER 3: FISH AND SEAFOOD   **15**

CHAPTER 4: VEGETABLES   **22**

CHAPTER 5: LAMB   **29**

CHAPTER 6: BEEF   **37**

CHAPTER 7: PORK   **44**

CHAPTER 8: POULTRY   **51**

CHAPTER 9: SNACK   **58**

CHAPTER 10: DESSERT   **65**

APPENDIX 1: 4-WEEK MEAL PLAN   **73**

APPENDIX 2: BASIC KITCHEN CONVERSIONS & EQUIVALENTS   **74**

APPENDIX 3: RECIPES INDEX   **75**

INTRODUCTION

Have you ever found yourself in the throes of a hectic day, craving a home-cooked meal but bogged down by the time constraints of modern life? I've been there. The struggle to balance a desire for wholesome, delicious meals with the demands of a busy schedule can be overwhelming. That's why I turned to the Ninja Foodi Smart XL Pressure Cooker, and it's been a game-changer.

The Ninja Foodi Smart XL isn't just an appliance; it's a kitchen companion that understands the struggles of modern living. From the frustration of juggling multiple pots and pans to the desire for healthier alternatives to our favorite fried delights – this cooker has addressed it all.

As someone who's navigated the culinary landscape armed with the Ninja Foodi Smart XL, I've experimented with recipes for every occasion. From succulent roasts to crispy air-fried treats and even artisanal bread that would make a bakery blush – this cooker has become my secret weapon.

And now, I'm thrilled to share my culinary escapades with you through this cookbook. Dive into a collection of recipes crafted with care and precision, tailored specifically for the Ninja Foodi Smart XL. Whether you're a seasoned home chef or a kitchen novice, this cookbook is your passport to unlocking the full potential of your pressure cooker. From quick weeknight dinners to extravagant weekend feasts, I've curated a range of recipes that cater to various tastes, moods, and dietary preferences.

Join me on this flavorful experience where the Ninja Foodi Smart XL isn't just an appliance but a culinary ally, turning your kitchen into a haven of efficiency and delight. Let's make every meal an occasion worth savoring.

CHAPTER 1
NINJA FOODI SMART XL PRESSURE COOKER

Benefits of Ninja Foodi Smart Pressure

Cooker / 3

Ninja Foodi Smart XL Pressure Cooker Vs

Other Cookers / 4

Learn about the Control Panel / 4

How to Use the Slider and SmartLid / 6

Let's Get Cooking! / 6

Meet the culinary powerhouse, the Ninja OL701 Foodi 14-in-1 SMART XL 8 Qt. Pressure Cooker Steam Fryer, complete with the innovative SmartLid and Thermometer for precision cooking. With its Auto-Steam Release and the ability to air fry, proof, and more, this kitchen marvel is designed to elevate your cooking experience. Featuring a generous 3-layer capacity and a 5 Qt. Crisp Basket, this Silver/Black beauty is not just a pressure cooker; it's a versatile culinary companion ready to tackle an array of cooking tasks with efficiency and style. Get ready to redefine your kitchen game with this Ninja Foodi – where smart technology meets culinary excellence.

Benefits of Ninja Foodi Smart Pressure Cooker

The Ninja Foodi Smart XL Pressure Cooker offers a range of benefits that make it a versatile and efficient kitchen appliance:

•Extra-Large Capacity
The family-sized capacity of the Ninja Foodi Smart XL allows for cooking large meals, making it ideal for families or gatherings. Its ability to perform pressure cooking, air frying, and SteamCrisp functions all under one SmartLid adds to its versatility.

•Foodi Smart Thermometer
The inclusion of the Foodi Smart Thermometer enhances cooking precision by providing accurate temperature readings at the touch of a button. This eliminates guesswork, ensuring that your dishes are cooked to perfection.

•Smart Cook System
The Smart Cook System features four smart protein settings and nine customizable doneness levels, allowing you to achieve the perfect cooking results, ranging from rare to well done. The three auto-steam release controls further enhance customization by allowing you to select your preferred pressure release setting.

•SmartLid Slider
The SmartLid Slider simplifies operation by allowing you to easily unlock three cooking modes and access 14 cooking functions, all conveniently housed under one lid. This streamlined design promotes user-friendly and efficient cooking.

•SteamCrisp Technology
The SteamCrisp Technology sets the Ninja Foodi Smart XL apart by enabling simultaneous steaming and crisping. This results in faster, juicier, and crispier outcomes without the risk of drying out, providing a significant advantage compared to other models that operate in dry mode only.

•Deluxe Reversible Rack
The inclusion of the Deluxe Reversible Rack adds to the cooker's flexibility by doubling cooking capacity or allowing you to prepare three-component full meals with mains and sides simultaneously. This feature enhances efficiency and convenience in meal preparation.

•Faster Cooking
The Ninja Foodi Smart XL stands out for its speed, offering up to 70% faster cooking than traditional

slow cooking methods. Additionally, it provides 40% faster 1-touch meals compared to traditional cooking methods and achieves 25% faster results in baking artisan bread and cakes when compared to conventional ovens. This time-saving aspect makes it a valuable tool for those seeking efficient meal preparation without compromising on quality.

Ninja Foodi Smart XL Pressure Cooker Vs Other Cookers

The Ninja Foodi Smart XL Pressure Cooker with SmartLid stands out for its multifunctionality, smart cooking features, and innovative technologies like SteamCrisp. These aspects differentiate it from many traditional pressure cookers, offering you a more versatile and efficient cooking experience.

Versatility:
This Ninja Foodi Smart XL model offers an extra-large capacity and combines pressure cooking, air frying, and SteamCrisp functions in one appliance, providing a wide range of cooking options. Many traditional pressure cookers may only offer pressure cooking functionality, lacking the versatility of additional cooking methods like air frying and Steam-Crisp.

Smart Cooking Technology:
Features a Smart Cook System with four protein settings, nine doneness levels, and three auto-steam release controls for precise and customizable cooking. Some pressure cookers may lack advanced smart cooking technologies, offering fewer customization options for achieving specific results.

SmartLid Slider:
The SmartLid Slider simplifies cooking with easy access to three cooking modes and 14 functions, consolidating multiple capabilities under one lid for convenience. Many traditional pressure cookers may not have a slider mechanism or may offer fewer cooking modes, potentially requiring you to switch lids or accessories for different functions.

SteamCrisp Technology:
The inclusion of SteamCrisp Technology allows for simultaneous steaming and crisping, resulting in faster, juicier, and crispier outcomes. Most traditional pressure cookers do not have dedicated technology for simultaneous steaming and crisping, potentially limiting the range of textures and flavors achievable.

Deluxe Reversible Rack:
The Ninja Foodi Smart XL cooker includes a Deluxe Reversible Rack that doubles cooking capacity or facilitates the preparation of three-component meals simultaneously. Many standard pressure cookers may lack a reversible rack or similar feature, limiting their ability to cook multiple items at once.

Cooking Speed:
The Ninja Foodi Smart XL offers faster cooking times, with up to 70% faster cooking than slow cooking methods, 40% faster 1-touch meals compared to traditional methods, and 25% faster baking of artisan bread and cakes than conventional ovens. While pressure cookers, in general, are known for faster cooking, the Ninja Foodi Smart XL emphasizes speed across a variety of cooking methods.

Learn about the Control Panel

Cooking Functions
The Ninja Foodi Smart XL Pressure Cooker boasts an array of cooking functions designed to cater to a diverse range of culinary needs.

PRESSURE:
The pressure function enables rapid cooking by utilizing high pressure, ensuring that dishes are prepared swiftly while retaining their tenderness. It is particularly well-suited for recipes that benefit from quick cooking without compromising on moisture or flavor.

STEAM & CRISP:
This one-touch function simplifies the creation of complete meals, offering a perfect balance of juicy and crisp textures for vegetables, proteins, and artisan breads. It's an ideal choice for those seeking a has-

sle-free way to achieve a harmonious combination of moist and crispy elements in their dishes.

STEAM & BAKE:
Tailored for baking enthusiasts, the steam and bake function facilitates the creation of fluffier cakes and quick breads in less time and with reduced fat. It is a valuable option for those who prioritize achieving a lighter texture in their baked goods.

AIR FRY:
The air fry function is designed to impart a crispy and crunchy texture to food using minimal to no oil. It provides a healthier alternative for those who enjoy the texture of fried foods but want to reduce their oil intake.

BROIL:
Employing high heat from above, the broil function is perfect for caramelizing and browning the tops of various dishes. It serves as a useful tool for putting the finishing touch on casseroles, meats, and other dishes, adding a delightful visual and textural appeal.

BAKE/ROAST:
Operating akin to an oven, the bake/roast function accommodates the preparation of tender meats, baked treats, and more. This versatile option allows you to bake and roast a variety of dishes without the need for a traditional oven.

DEHYDRATE:
The dehydrate function is geared towards crafting healthy snacks by removing moisture from meats, fruits, and vegetables. It provides an effective means of preserving food while retaining its nutritional value, allowing for the creation of items like dried fruits and jerky.

PROOF:
For those engaged in the art of baking, the proof function creates an optimal environment for dough to rest and rise, an essential step in ensuring the success of bread and pizza dough before they hit the oven.

SEAR/SAUTÉ:
Serving as a stovetop substitute, the sear/sauté function allows for the browning of meats, sautéing of vegetables, simmering of sauces, and more. It provides a convenient all-in-one solution for pre-cooking steps within the same appliance.

STEAM:
The steam function delicately cooks sensitive foods at a high temperature, making it an ideal choice for

vegetables, seafood, or other items that benefit from gentle steam cooking.

SOUS VIDE:
Rooted in the French term meaning "under vacuum," the sous vide function enables slow cooking of food sealed in a plastic bag within a precisely regulated water bath. This method ensures precise and consistent results for slow-cooked dishes.

SLOW COOK:
Tailored for those who appreciate the flavors that develop over time, the slow cook function allows food to be cooked at a lower temperature for an extended period. It's perfect for simmering stews, soups, and other dishes, allowing flavors to meld and intensify gradually.

YOGURT:
It not only pasteurizes the milk but also ferments it to perfection, giving you that delightful homemade yogurt taste.

KEEP WARM:
The unit automatically switches to "keep warm" after every cooking cycle. No worries, though! If you want to take control, just hit the Keep Warm button after starting a function to disable this automatic transition.

Operating Buttons

SMARTLID SLIDER:
This slider is like your magic wand! As you move it, the available functions for each mode light up, making it easy-peasy to switch between cooking modes.

DIAL:
Once you've chosen a mode with the slider, use the dial to scroll through the available functions until you find the one that fits your culinary dreams.

LEFT ARROWS:

Those handy up/down arrows on the left of the display? Use them to adjust cooking temperature or set internal doneness for PRESET and Manual buttons.

RIGHT ARROWS:

Now, the up/down arrows on the right of the display? They're your friends for adjusting cooking time or setting the food type when using PRESET. Super versatile!

PRESET:

Want a bit of help? The PRESET button switches the display so you can set the thermometer, food type, and internal doneness based on preset temperatures. Except for some functions like Dehydrate, Sous Vide, Proof, Steam, and Slow Cook, where it sits back and lets you take control.

MANUAL:

Feeling hands-on? The MANUAL button is your ticket to manually set the thermometer's target internal temperature. It's not available for some functions, like Dehydrate, Sous Vide, and Slow Cook, but it's ready to roll for most others.

START/STOP BUTTON:

Press this button, and you're off to the races! Start your cooking adventure, and if you need to take a pause, press it again to stop the current cooking function.

(POWER) BUTTON:

Last but not least, the Power button is your all-stop shop. Press it, and the unit shuts off, bringing all cooking modes to a halt. It's like hitting the reset button for culinary creativity.

How to Use the Slider and SmartLid

The SmartLid Slider on the Ninja Foodi Smart XL Pressure Cooker serves as a crucial mechanism for switching between different cooking modes and communicating the chosen function to the lid. It provides you with the flexibility to select from three distinct cooking modes:

• PRESSURE: This mode is specifically designed for pressure cooking, ensuring that the appliance can operate under high pressure for certain recipes.

• STEAMCRISP:The STEAMCRISP mode is tailored for simultaneous steaming and crisping, allowing you to achieve juicier and crispier results with certain dishes.

•AIR FRY/STOVETOP: In this mode, you can utilize the unit for air frying, giving their dishes a crispy texture, or use it as a stovetop for traditional cooking methods.

How to Open & Close the Lid:

Proper handling of the Ninja Foodi Smart XL lid is crucial for safe and efficient cooking. You should consistently use the handle positioned above the SmartLid Slider for both opening and closing the lid. This designated handle ensures a secure grip and smooth operation. The lid can be used, i.e., opened and closed, when the slider is in the STEAMCRISP and AIR FRY/STOVETOP positions. These positions enable you to access the interior of the appliance for loading and unloading ingredients.

Pressure Position:

To maintain safety during pressure cooking, the lid is intentionally designed to be non-operable when the slider is in the PRESSURE position. This precautionary measure prevents accidental opening while pressure is built up inside the unit.

Non-Pressure Modes:

When there is no pressure in the unit, you can safely move the slider to the STEAMCRISP or AIR FRY/STOVETOP position to open the lid. This step ensures that you can access the cooking chamber without compromising safety.

Let's Get Cooking!

Let's make the most of your Ninja OL701 Foodi 14-in-1 SMART XL 8 Qt. Pressure Cooker Steam Fryer with SmartLid. Unbox your Ninja OL701 and acquaint yourself with its components: the main unit, SmartLid, pressure cooker lid, and accessories. Take a moment to review the user manual for specific guidelines.

1.SmartLid Setup

Attach the SmartLid to the unit, ensuring a secure fit. The SmartLid is your gateway to diverse cooking modes, so make sure it's in place before you dive into your culinary exploits.

2.Plug it In

Connect your Ninja Foodi to a power source. This cooker is ready to roll once it's plugged in and powered up.

3.Explore the SmartLid Slider

Take note of the SmartLid Slider. As you move it, different cooking modes will light up. It's like your menu selector, allowing you to choose the function that suits your culinary desires.

4.Choose a Cooking Mode

Select your preferred cooking mode by moving the slider to the appropriate setting. Whether you're craving pressure-cooked perfection, steamy goodness, or the crispiness of air frying, the SmartLid has you covered.

5.Adjust Settings

Once you've chosen a mode, use the dial to scroll through available functions until your desired one is highlighted. Adjust the cooking time or temperature using the arrows on the display to achieve the precise outcome you're aiming for.

6.Start Cooking

Press the START/STOP button to kick off your cooking adventure. Your Ninja OL701 will take it from here, bringing your culinary vision to life.

7.Keep an Eye (and Ear) Out

As your dish progresses, pay attention to the sounds and aromas emanating from your Ninja Foodi. It's all part of the sensory experience, and you'll become attuned to the delightful cues indicating your meal's progress.

8.Enjoy the Feast

Once the cooking cycle is complete, open the lid using the handle above the slider. Take in the tantalizing aroma, and voilà! Your culinary creation is ready to be savored.

CHAPTER 2
BREAKFAST

Ginger Chicken Porridge / 9

Bacon and Spinach Cups / 9

Cornflakes Toast Sticks / 10

Macaroni and Cheese / 10

Greek Pumpkin Bread / 11

Dill Zucchini Fritters / 11

Bacon Wrapped Sausage / 12

British Scotch Eggs / 12

Veggie Frittata / 13

Sweet Potato Hash / 13

Creamy Parsley Soufflé / 13

Mediterranean Spinach Strata / 14

Homemade Refried Black Beans / 14

Nutty Baked Apples / 14

Ginger Chicken Porridge

SERVES: 8

PREP: 10 minutes
TOTAL COOK TIME: 30 minutes
PRESSURE BUILD: approx. 15 minutes
COOK: 15 minutes

2 cups medium-grain white rice
2 pounds (907 g) boneless, skinless chicken thighs
1 (2-inch) piece fresh ginger, peeled and minced
2 tbsps. kosher salt

1. Add the rice, chicken, and ginger to the pot and fill with enough water to the fill line.
2. Close lid and move slider to PRESSURE. Make sure the pressure release valve is in the SEAL position.
3. The temperature will default to HIGH, which is the correct setting. Select DELAYED RELEASE. Set time to 15 minutes. Select START/STOP to begin cooking (the unit will build pressure for approx. 15 minutes before cooking begins).
4. When pressure cooking is complete, the unit will naturally release pressure for 10 minutes. After 10 minutes, quick release any remaining pressure by moving the pressure release valve to the VENT position. Select START/STOP and move slider to either STEAM-CRISP or AIR FRY/STOVETOP to unlock the lid, then carefully open it.
5. Stir in the salt. Let the congee cool in the pot for about 10 minutes, and stir frequently.
6. Ladle the congee into bowls and serve warm.

Bacon and Spinach Cups

SERVES: 4

PREP: 15 minutes
TOTAL COOK TIME: 35 minutes
STEAM: approx. 20 minutes
COOK: 15 minutes

1 cup water, for steaming
cooking spray
6 large eggs
¾ cup mozzarella cheese, shredded
2 tbsps. heavy whipping cream
½ cup red peppers, chopped
¼ cup fresh spinach, chopped
3 slices bacon, cooked and crumbled
Salt and black pepper, to taste

1. Pour 1 cup water into the pot. Spray 4 silicone molds with cooking spray.
2. In a large bowl, whisk together eggs with cream, salt and black pepper until combined.
3. Stir in the remaining ingredients and transfer the mixture into silicone molds.
4. Place the silicone molds on the bottom rack, then place the rack in the pot. Close the lid and move slider to STEAMCRISP.
5. Select STEAM & BAKE, set temperature to 350°F, and set time to 15 minutes. Press START/STOP to begin cooking (PrE will display for approx. 20 minutes as the unit steams, then the timer will start counting down).
6. When cooking is complete, remove the rack with the silicone molds and let cool for 10 minutes. Serve warm.

Cornflakes Toast Sticks

SERVES: 4

PREP TIME: 10 minutes
COOK TIME: 12 minutes

Cooking spray
6 slices sandwich bread, each slice cut into 4 strips
2 eggs
½ cup milk
¾ cup crushed cornflakes
⅛ tsp. salt
½ tsp. pure vanilla extract
Maple syrup, for dipping

1. Close the lid and move slider to the AIR FRY/STOVETOP. Preheat the pot by selecting AIR FRY, setting temperature to 390°F, and setting time to 5 minutes. Select START/STOP to begin preheating.
2. While unit is preheating, beat together the eggs, milk, salt, and vanilla in a small bowl.
3. Place the crushed cornflakes on a plate.
4. Dunk the bread strips in egg mixture, shake off excess, and roll in cornflake crumbs.
5. Spray both sides of bread strips with cooking spray.
6. Attach Cook & Crisp Basket with diffuser and add the bread strips in a single layer.
7. When the pot has preheated, place the basket in the pot. Close the lid and make sure the slider is still in the AIR FRY/STOVETOP.
8. Select AIR FRY, set temperature to 390°F, and set time to 6 minutes. Select START/STOP to begin cooking.
9. Repeat with the remaining toast sticks.
10. When cooking is complete, remove the basket and serve the toast sticks with maple syrup.

Macaroni and Cheese

SERVES: 6

PREP: 10 minutes
TOTAL COOK TIME: 15 minutes
PRESSURE BUILD: approx. 12 minutes
COOK: 3 minutes

1 (1-pound, 454 g) box elbow macaroni
2 large eggs
10 ounces (283 g) mild cheddar cheese, shredded (about 2½ cups)
¾ cup heavy cream
3 tbsps. unsalted butter
1 tsp. dry mustard
1½ tsps. kosher salt
Freshly ground black pepper

1. Add the macaroni to the pot. Fill with enough water to cover the pasta.
2. Close lid and move slider to PRESSURE. Make sure the pressure release valve is in the SEAL position.
3. The temperature will default to HIGH, which is the correct setting. Select DELAYED RELEASE. Set time to 0 minutes. Select START/STOP to begin cooking (the unit will build pressure for approx. 12 minutes before cooking begins).
4. When pressure cooking is complete, the unit will naturally release pressure for 10 minutes. After 10 minutes, quick release any remaining pressure by moving the pressure release valve to the VENT position. Select START/STOP and move slider to either STEAMCRISP or AIR FRY/STOVETOP to unlock the lid, then carefully open it. Stir the butter into the macaroni.
5. Whisk together the eggs, cream, mustard, and salt in a mixing bowl.
6. Keep slider in the AIR FRY/STOVETOP position. Select SEAR/SAUTÉ and set t0 3. Add the egg mixture and cheese to the pot, stir until the cheese is entirely melted.
7. Season with some black pepper. Serve warm.

Greek Pumpkin Bread

SERVES: 4

PREP: 10 minutes
TOTAL COOK TIME: 35 minutes
STEAM: approx. 20 minutes
COOK: 15 minutes

1 cup water, for steaming
cooking spray
2 large eggs
8 tbsps. pumpkin puree
6 tbsps. oats
6 tbsps. banana flour
4 tbsps. honey
4 tbsps. plain Greek yogurt
2 tbsps. vanilla essence
Pinch of ground nutmeg

1. Pour 1 cup water into the pot. Spray a loaf pan with cooking spray.
2. Mix together all the ingredients except the oats in a bowl and beat with the hand mixer until smooth. Add the oats and mix until well combined.
3. Transfer the oat mixture into the prepared loaf pan.
4. Place the pan on the bottom rack, then place the rack in the pot. Close the lid and move slider to STEAMCRISP.
5. Select STEAM & BAKE, set temperature to 350°F, and set time to 15 minutes. Press START/STOP to begin cooking (PrE will display for approx. 20 minutes as the unit steams, then the timer will start counting down).
6. When cooking is complete, remove the rack with the pan and let cool for 10 minutes. Cut the bread into desired size slices to serve.

Dill Zucchini Fritters

SERVES: 4

PREP: 15 minutes
TOTAL COOK TIME: 16 minutes
STEAM: approx. 6 minutes
COOK: 10 minutes

½ cup water, for steaming
2 eggs
10½ ounces zucchini, grated and squeezed
7 ounces Halloumi cheese
¼ cup all-purpose flour
1 tsp. fresh dill, minced
Salt and black pepper, to taste

1. Mix together all the ingredients in a large bowl. Shape the mixture into small fritters.
2. Add ½ cup water to the pot. Spray the Cook & Crisp Basket with cooking spray, then place the basket in the pot. Add the fritters to the basket, spreading it evenly across the basket. Close the lid and move slider to STEAMCRISP.
3. Select STEAM & CRISP, set temperature to 360°F, and set time to 10 minutes. Press START/STOP to begin cooking (PrE will display for approx. 6 minutes as the unit steams, then the timer will start counting down).
4. With 5 minutes remaining, open the lid and flip the fritters with tongs. Close the lid to continue cooking.
5. When the cooking is complete, remove the basket from pot. Transfer the fritters to a plate and serve warm.

Bacon Wrapped Sausage

SERVES: 3

PREP TIME: 5 minutes
COOK TIME: 10 minutes

9 slices bacon
3 brazilian sausages, cut into 3 equal pieces
1 tbsp. Italian herbs
Salt and ground black pepper, to taste

1. Wrap each piece of sausage with a slice of bacon. Sprinkle with Italian herbs, salt and black pepper.
2. Close the lid and move slider to the AIR FRY/STOVETOP. Preheat the pot by selecting AIR FRY, setting temperature to 390°F, and setting time to 5 minutes. Select START/STOP to begin preheating.
3. While unit is preheating, wrap each piece of sausage with a slice of bacon. Sprinkle with Italian herbs, salt and black pepper.
4. Attach Cook & Crisp Basket with diffuser and add the sausages.
5. When the pot has preheated, place the basket in the pot. Close the lid and make sure the slider is still in the AIR FRY/STOVETOP.
6. Select AIR FRY, set temperature to 390°F, and set time to 10 minutes. Select START/STOP to begin cooking, flipping halfway through cooking.
7. When cooking is complete, remove the basket and serve the sausages warm.

British Scotch Eggs

SERVES: 4

PREP TIME: 5 minutes
COOK TIME: 28 minutes

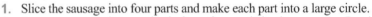

cooking spray
1 (12-ounce / 340-g) package pork sausage
4 large hard boiled eggs
8 slices thick-cut bacon
Special Equipment:
4 wooden toothpicks, soaked in water for at least 30 minutes

1. Slice the sausage into four parts and make each part into a large circle.
2. Arrange an egg into each circle and wrap it in the sausage. Put in the refrigerator for 1 hour.
3. Close the lid and move slider to the AIR FRY/STOVETOP. Preheat the pot by selecting BAKE/ROAST, setting temperature to 400°F, and setting time to 5 minutes. Select START/STOP to begin preheating.
4. While unit is preheating, spray the Ninja Multi-Purpose Pan with cooking spray.
5. Make a cross with two pieces of thick-cut bacon. Put a wrapped egg in the center, fold the bacon over top of the egg, and secure with a toothpick. Arrange the eggs on the prepared pan.
6. Place the pan on the bottom rack. When the pot has preheated, place the rack with pan in the pot. Close the lid and make sure the slider is still in the AIR FRY/STOVETOP.
7. Select BAKE/ROAST, set temperature to 400°F, and set time to 28 minutes. Select START/STOP to begin cooking, flipping halfway through cooking.
8. When cooking is complete, remove the rack with the pan and let cool for 10 minutes. Serve immediately.

Veggie Frittata

PREP: 10 minutes	1 cup water, for steaming	¼ cup spinach, chopped
TOTAL COOK TIME: 35 minutes	1 tbsp. butter	2 green onions, chopped
STEAM: approx. 20 minutes	4 eggs	½ tsp. salt
COOK: 15 minutes	½ cup milk	½ tsp. black pepper
	¼ cup baby Bella mushrooms, chopped	Dash of hot sauce

1. Pour 1 cup water into the pot. Spray the bottom of the Ninja Multi-Purpose Pan with butter, avoiding the sides.
2. Whisk the eggs with milk in a large bowl and toss in the chopped green onions, mushrooms and spinach.
3. Sprinkle with salt, pepper and hot sauce and pour this mixture into the prepared pan.
4. Place the pan on the bottom rack, then place the rack in the pot. Close the lid and move slider to STEAMCRISP.
5. Select STEAM & BAKE, set temperature to 350°F, and set time to 15 minutes. Press START/STOP to begin cooking (PrE will display for approx. 20 minutes as the unit steams, then the timer will start counting down).
6. When cooking is complete, remove the rack with the pan and let cool for about 5 minutes. Serve warm.

Sweet Potato Hash

SERVES: 6

PREP: 10 minutes	½ cup water, for steaming	1 tbsp. smoked paprika
TOTAL COOK TIME: 19 minutes	2 tbsps. olive oil	1 tsp. dried dill weed
STEAM: approx. 6 minutes	2 large sweet potato, cut into small cubes	1 tsp. sea salt
COOK: 13 minutes	2 slices bacon, cut into small pieces	1 tsp. ground black pepper

1. Mix together olive oil, sweet potato, bacon, paprika, salt, black pepper and dill in a large bowl.
2. Add ½ cup water to the pot and place the Cook & Crisp Basket in the pot. Transfer the sweet potato mixture in the basket. Close the lid and move slider to STEAMCRISP.
3. Select STEAM & CRISP, set temperature to 390°F, and set time to 13 minutes. Press START/STOP to begin cooking (PrE will display for approx. 6 minutes as the unit steams, then the timer will start counting down).
4. With 5 minutes remaining, open the lid and toss the mixture with tongs. Close the lid to continue cooking.
5. When the cooking is complete, remove the basket from pot. Serve warm.

Creamy Parsley Soufflé

SERVES: 2

PREP: 5 minutes	1 cup water, for steaming
TOTAL COOK TIME: 30 minutes	cooking spray
STEAM: approx. 20 minutes	2 eggs
COOK: 10 minutes	1 fresh red chili pepper, chopped
	2 tbsps. light cream
	1 tbsp. fresh parsley, chopped
	Salt, to taste

1. Pour 1 cup water into the pot. Spray 2 soufflé dishes with cooking spray.
2. In a bowl, mix together all the ingredients until well combined.
3. Transfer the egg mixture into prepared soufflé dishes.
4. Place the soufflé dishes on the bottom rack, then place the rack in the pot. Close the lid and move slider to STEAMCRISP.
5. Select STEAM & BAKE, set temperature to 350°F, and set time to 10 minutes. Press START/STOP to begin cooking (PrE will display for approx. 20 minutes as the unit steams, then the timer will start counting down).
6. When cooking is complete, remove the rack with the soufflé dishes and serve warm.

Mediterranean Spinach Strata

PREP TIME: 16 minutes COOK TIME: 6 hours	2 tbsps. olive oil 8 cups whole-wheat bread, cut into cubes 4 eggs 2 egg whites 2 red bell peppers, stemmed, seeded, and chopped	2 cups chopped baby spinach leaves 1 onion, finely chopped 1½ cups 2% milk 1 cup shredded Asiago cheese 3 garlic cloves, minced

1. Mix the bread cubes, bell peppers, spinach, onion and garlic in the pot.
2. In a medium bowl, mix the olive oil, eggs, egg whites, and milk, then beat well. Add this egg mixture into the pot. Top with the cheese.
3. Close the lid and move slider to AIR FRY/STOVETOP. Select SLOW COOK, set temperature to Lo, and set time to 6 hours. Press START/STOP to begin cooking, until a food thermometer registers 165°F and the strata is set and puffed.
4. When cooking is complete, let cool for 5 minutes and serve warm.

Homemade Refried Black Beans

PREP: 10 minutes TOTAL COOK TIME: 55 minutes PRESSURE BUILD: approx. 15 minutes COOK: 40 minutes	2 tbsps. peanut oil or vegetable oil 1 pound (454 g) dried black beans, rinsed and picked through for debris 4 cups water	½ medium yellow onion, diced 2 garlic cloves, minced 1 tsp. ground cumin 1 tsp. kosher salt, plus more as needed

1. Add the beans, cumin, onion, garlic, salt, and 4 cups water to the pot.
2. Close lid and move slider to PRESSURE. Make sure the pressure release valve is in the SEAL position.
3. The temperature will default to HIGH, which is the correct setting. Select DELAYED RELEASE. Set time to 30 minutes. Select START/STOP to begin cooking (the unit will build pressure for approx. 15 minutes before cooking begins).
4. When pressure cooking is complete, the unit will naturally release pressure for 10 minutes. After 10 minutes, quick release any remaining pressure by moving the pressure release valve to the VENT position. Select START/STOP and move slider to either STEAMCRISP or AIR FRY/STOVETOP to unlock the lid, then carefully open it.
5. Add the oil and mash the beans with a silicone potato masher, until they are smooth.
6. Keep slider in the AIR FRY/STOVETOP position. Select SEAR/SAUTÉ and set to Hi5. Cook for about 10 minutes. Stir well and mash every couple of minutes.
7. Season with salt to taste before serving.

Nutty Baked Apples

PREP TIME: 15 minutes COOK TIME: 5 hours	6 tbsps. unsalted butter, cut into pieces 8 large apples ½ cup apple juice 1½ cups buckwheat flakes 1 cup chopped walnuts	⅓ cup coconut sugar 2 tbsps. freshly squeezed lemon juice 1 tsp. ground cinnamon ¼ tsp. salt

1. Peel a strip of skin around the top of each apple to prevent splitting. Gently remove the apple core, making sure not to cut all the way through to the bottom. Coat the apples with the lemon juice and set aside.
2. Mix the walnuts, buckwheat flakes, coconut sugar, cinnamon, and salt in a medium bowl.
3. Pour the melted butter over the buckwheat mixture and combine until crumbly. Stuff the apples with this mixture, rounding the stuffing on top of each apple.
4. Arrange the stuffed apples in the pot. Add the apple juice around the apples.
5. Close the lid and move slider to AIR FRY/STOVETOP. Select SLOW COOK, set temperature to Buffet, and set time to 5 hours. Press START/STOP to begin cooking, until the apples are very soft.
6. When cooking is complete, let cool for about 5 minutes and serve warm.

CHAPTER 3
FISH AND SEAFOOD

Breaded Hake and Green Beans Meal / 16

Chinese-style Glazed Cod / 16

Garlic Squid / 17

Cajun Spiced Salmon / 17

Crispy Nacho Prawns / 18

Buttered Scallops / 18

Italian Salmon Patties / 19

Seasoned Crab Sticks / 19

Inspired Halibut / 19

Salmon, Mushroom and Barley / 20

Spanish Garlic Shrimp / 20

Creamy Penne and Tuna Cakes / 21

Garlic Lemon Butter Seared Scallops / 21

Breaded Hake and Green Beans Meal

SERVES: 2

PREP: 25 minutes
TOTAL COOK TIME: 27 minutes
STEAM: approx. 15 minutes
COOK: 12 minutes

LEVEL 1 (BOTTOM OF POT)
2 cups water
1 cup white rice, rinsed
LEVEL 2 (BOTTOM RACK)
1 cup green beans
Kosher salt, as desired
Ground black pepper, as desired

LEVEL 3 (TOP RACK)
2 tbsps. vegetable oil
4 (6-ounces) hake fillets
4 ounces breadcrumbs
1 egg
1 lemon, cut into wedges

1. Place all Level 1 ingredients in the pot and stir until evenly combined.
2. Place all Level 2 ingredients in a large bowl and stir until combined. Cover the bottom rack with aluminum foil, then place the rack in the pot. Place the green beans on top of the foil.
3. Whisk the egg in a shallow bowl and combine the breadcrumbs and oil in another bowl.
4. Dip the hake fillets into the whisked egg and then, dredge in the breadcrumb mixture.
5. Place the top rack in the pot. Place the hake fillets on the top rack. Close the lid and move slider to STEAMCRISP.
6. Select STEAM & CRISP, set temperature to 350°F, and set time to 12 minutes. Press START/STOP to begin cooking (PrE will display for approx. 15 minutes as the unit steams, then the timer will start counting down).
7. When cooking is complete, remove the rack with the hake fillets, then the rack with the green beans. Stir the rice and serve warm with hake fillets and green beans.

Chinese-style Glazed Cod

SERVES: 2

PREP: 20 minutes
TOTAL COOK TIME: 16 minutes
STEAM: approx. 6 minutes
COOK: 10 minutes

½ cup water, for steaming
4 (3½-ounces) cod fillets
⅓ cup honey
⅓ cup soy sauce
3 tsps. rice wine vinegar
1 tsp. water

1. Mix the honey soy sauce,, vinegar and 1 tsp. water in a small bowl. Reserve about half of the mixture in another bowl.
2. Stir the cod fillets in the remaining mixture until evenly coated. Cover and refrigerate to marinate for about 3 hours.
3. Add ½ cup water to the pot. Spray the Cook & Crisp Basket with cooking spray, then place the basket in the pot. Add the cod fillets to the basket. Close the lid and move slider to STEAMCRISP.
4. Select STEAM & CRISP, set temperature to 450°F, and set time to 10 minutes. Press START/STOP to begin cooking (PrE will display for approx. 6 minutes as the unit steams, then the timer will start counting down).
5. With 5 minutes remaining, open the lid and flip the cod with tongs. Close the lid to continue cooking.
6. When the cooking is complete, remove the basket from pot. Transfer the cod to a plate. Coat evenly with the reserved marinade and serve hot.

Garlic Squid

SERVES: 4

PREP TIME: 10 minutes
COOK TIME: 2 hours

4 small clean squids
2 tbsps. olive oil
2 garlic cloves, chopped
Salt and pepper to taste
lemon juice for serving

1. Add 12 cups of room-temperature water to the pot.
2. Close the lid and move slider to AIR FRY/STOVETOP, then use the dial to select SOUS VIDE. Select SOUS VIDE, set temperature to 130°F, and set time to 2 hours.
3. Press START/STOP to begin preheating.
4. Season the squid with salt and put into a Sous Vide bag. Add the olive oil and chopped garlic.
5. When preheating is complete and "ADD FOOD" will show on the display.
6. Open the lid and place bag in the water using the water displacement method. When just the bag's seal is above the water line, finish closing the bag, making sure no water gets inside. Keep the bag's seal just above the water line. Close the lid.
7. When cooking is complete, remove the bag with squid from cooker.
8. Serve sprinkled with lemon juice.

Cajun Spiced Salmon

SERVES: 2

PREP TIME: 10 minutes
COOK TIME: 10 minutes

cooking spray
2 (7-ounces) (¾-inch thick) salmon fillets
1 tbsp. fresh lemon juice
1 tbsp. Cajun seasoning
½ tsp. coconut sugar

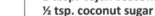

1. Close the lid and move slider to the AIR FRY/STOVETOP. Preheat the pot by selecting BAKE/ROAST, setting temperature to 390°F, and setting time to 5 minutes. Select START/STOP to begin preheating.
2. While unit is preheating, season the salmon with Cajun seasoning and coconut sugar.
3. Spray the salmon with cooking spray and place on the bottom rack.
4. When the pot has preheated, place the rack with salmon in the pot. Close the lid and make sure the slider is still in the AIR FRY/STOVETOP.
5. Select BAKE/ROAST, set temperature to 390°F, and set time to 10 minutes. Select START/STOP to begin cooking, flipping halfway through cooking.
6. When cooking is complete, remove the rack with salmon and let cool for 5 minutes. Drizzle with the lemon juice and serve hot.

Crispy Nacho Prawns

PREP TIME: 15 minutes
COOK TIME: 10 minutes

cooking spray
18 prawns, peeled and deveined
½ pound nacho chips, crushed
1 egg
Salt and black pepper, to taste

1. Close the lid and move slider to the AIR FRY/STOVETOP. Preheat the pot by selecting AIR FRY, setting temperature to 390°F, and setting time to 5 minutes. Select START/STOP to begin preheating.
2. While unit is preheating, crack the egg in a shallow dish and beat well.
3. Add the crushed nacho chips in another shallow dish.
4. Coat the prawns with egg, salt and black pepper, then roll into nacho chips.
5. When the pot has preheated, spray the racks with cooking spray. Place the bottom rack in the pot and arrange half of prawns. Place the top rack on the pot and put the remaining half of prawns.
6. Close the lid and make sure the slider is still in the AIR FRY/STOVETOP.
7. Select AIR FRY, set temperature to 390°F, and set time to 10 minutes. Select START/STOP to begin cooking, tossing halfway through cooking.
8. When cooking is complete, remove the racks and transfer the prawns to a plate. Serve hot.

Buttered Scallops

PREP TIME: 15 minutes
COOK TIME: 6 minutes

cooking spray
1 tbsp. butter, melted
¾ pound sea scallops, cleaned and patted very dry
½ tbsp. fresh thyme, minced
Salt and black pepper, as required

1. Close the lid and move slider to the AIR FRY/STOVETOP. Preheat the pot by selecting AIR FRY, setting temperature to 390°F, and setting time to 5 minutes. Select START/STOP to begin preheating.
2. While unit is preheating, mix the scallops, butter, thyme, salt, and pepper in a bowl.
3. Attach Cook & Crisp Basket with diffuser and spray with cooking spray, then add the scallops in a single layer.
4. When the pot has preheated, place the basket in the pot. Close the lid and make sure the slider is still in the AIR FRY/STOVETOP.
5. Select AIR FRY, set temperature to 390°F, and set time to 6 minutes. Select START/STOP to begin cooking, flipping halfway through cooking.
6. When cooking is complete, remove the basket and transfer the scallops in a platter. Serve hot.

Italian Salmon Patties

SERVES: 4

PREP: 10 minutes TOTAL COOK TIME: 8 minutes	Cooking spray 2 large eggs, beaten 2 (5-ounce / 142 g) cans salmon, flaked ⅔ cup panko bread crumbs	⅓ cup minced onion 1½ tsps. Italian-Style seasoning 1 tsp. garlic powder

1. Stir together the salmon, eggs and minced onion in a medium bowl.
2. Whisk the Italian-Style seasoning, bread crumbs, and garlic powder in a small bowl until blended well. Place the bread crumb mixture into the salmon mixture and stir well until blended. Form the salmon mixture into 8 patties.
3. Spray the bottom rack with cooking spray and arrange the patties. Place the rack with patties in the pot. Close the lid and move slider to the AIR FRY/STOVETOP.
4. Select BROIL, set temperature to 450°F, and time to 8 minutes. Press START/STOP to begin broiling. Halfway through cooking, flip the patties and lightly spritz with cooking spray.
5. When cooking is complete, transfer the patties to a plate and serve hot.

Seasoned Crab Sticks

SERVES: 4

PREP TIME: 10 minutes COOK TIME: 12 minutes	cooking spray 2 tsps. sesame oil 1 packet crab sticks, shred into small pieces Cajun seasoning, to taste

1. Close the lid and move slider to the AIR FRY/STOVETOP. Preheat the pot by selecting AIR FRY, setting temperature to 330°F, and setting time to 5 minutes. Select START/STOP to begin preheating.
2. While unit is preheating, drizzle the crab stick pieces with sesame oil.
3. Attach Cook & Crisp Basket with diffuser and spray with cooking spray, then add the crab stick pieces.
4. When the pot has preheated, place the basket in the pot. Close the lid and make sure the slider is still in the AIR FRY/STOVETOP.
5. Select AIR FRY, set temperature to 330°F, and set time to 12 minutes. Select START/STOP to begin cooking, tossing halfway through cooking.
6. When cooking is complete, remove the basket and serve sprinkled with Cajun seasoning.

Inspired Halibut

SERVES: 2

PREP TIME: 10 minutes COOK TIME: 15 minutes	1 tbsp. olive oil 2 (8-ounce / 227-g) halibut steaks ½ cup white wine ¼ cup butter 3 tbsps. capers, with liquid vinegar 1 tsp. chopped garlic Salt and pepper to taste

1. Close lid and move slider to AIR FRY/STOVETOP. Select SEAR/SAUTÉ and set to 4. Open lid and select START/STOP to begin preheating. Allow unit to preheat for 5 minutes.
2. After 5 minutes, add the olive oil to pot. Sear the halibut steaks until browned from all sides.
3. Transfer the halibut steaks into a bowl and set aside.
4. Pour in the wine and with a spatula scrape any browned bits from the bottom.
5. Cook until the wine is almost absorbed.
6. Toss in the butter, garlic, capers, salt and black pepper and simmer for about 1 minute.
7. Stir in the cooked steaks and cook until the fish flakes easily with a fork.
8. Transfer the steaks on a plate and serve immediately with the sauce from the pot poured over it.

Salmon, Mushroom and Barley

SERVES: 4 TO 6

PREP TIME: 9 minutes **COOK TIME:** 8½ hours	6 (5-ounce / 142-g) salmon fillets 2 cups hulled barley, rinsed 2 fennel bulbs, cored and chopped 2 red bell peppers, stemmed, seeded, and chopped 1 (8-ounce / 227-g) package cremini mushrooms, sliced 5 cups vegetable broth ⅓ cup grated Parmesan cheese 4 garlic cloves, minced 1 tsp. dried tarragon leaves ⅛ tsp. freshly ground black pepper

1. Mix the barley, fennel, mushrooms, bell peppers, garlic, vegetable broth, tarragon, and pepper in the pot.
2. Close the lid and move slider to AIR FRY/STOVETOP. Select SLOW COOK, set temperature to Lo, and set time to 8 hours. Press START/STOP to begin cooking, until the barley has absorbed most of the liquid and is soft, and the vegetables are soft too.
3. When cooking is complete, open the lid and top with the salmon fillets. Close the lid and cook on low for another 30 to 40 minutes, or until the salmon flakes when tested with a fork.
4. Toss in Parmesan cheese, breaking up the salmon, and serve hot.

Spanish Garlic Shrimp

SERVES: 4

PREP TIME: 10 minutes **COOK TIME:** 8 minutes	Cooking spray 12 ounces (340 g) medium shrimp, deveined, with tails on 2 tsps. olive oil 2 tsps. minced garlic 2 tsps. lemon juice ½ to 1 tsp. crushed red pepper

1. In a medium bowl, combine together the olive oil, lemon juice, garlic, and crushed red pepper to make a marinade.
2. Place the shrimp and toss to coat evenly with the marinade. Cover with plastic wrap and put the bowl in the refrigerator for about 30 minutes.
3. Close the lid and move slider to the AIR FRY/STOVETOP. Preheat the pot by selecting AIR FRY, setting temperature to 390°F, and setting time to 5 minutes. Select START/STOP to begin preheating.
4. While unit is preheating, attach Cook & Crisp Basket with diffuser and spray with cooking spray, then add the shrimp.
5. When the pot has preheated, place the basket in the pot. Close the lid and make sure the slider is still in the AIR FRY/STOVETOP.
6. Select AIR FRY, set temperature to 390°F, and set time to 8 minutes. Select START/STOP to begin cooking, flipping halfway through cooking.
7. When cooking is complete, remove the basket and let cool for 5 minutes before serving.

Creamy Penne and Tuna Cakes

SERVES: 4

PREP: 20 minutes
TOTAL COOK TIME: 27 minutes
STEAM: approx. 12 minutes
COOK: 15 minutes

LEVEL 1 (BOTTOM OF POT)
1 box (8 ounces) penne pasta
½ cup grated goat cheese
¼ cup cream
1½ cups water or chicken stock
LEVEL 2 (TOP RACK)
2 (6-ounces) cans tuna, drained
1½ tbsps. mayonnaise
1½ tbsps. almond flour
1 tbsp. fresh lemon juice
1 tsp. garlic powder
1 tsp. dried dill
½ tsp. onion powder
Pinch of salt and ground black pepper

1. Place all Level 1 ingredients in the pot and stir until combined.
2. Mix the tuna, almond flour, mayonnaise, lemon juice, dill, and spices in a large bowl.
3. Make 4 equal-sized patties from the tuna mixture.
4. Place the top rack in the pot, then place the patties on the rack. Close the lid and move slider to STEAMCRISP position.
5. Select STEAM & CRISP, set temperature to 350°F, and set time to 15 minutes. Press START/STOP to begin cooking (PrE will display for approx. 12 minutes as the unit steams, then the timer will start counting down).
6. When cooking is complete, remove the rack with the tuna cakes. Stir the cheese and serve with tuna cakes.

Garlic Lemon Butter Seared Scallops

SERVES: 4

PREP: 5 minutes
TOTAL COOK TIME: 27 minutes
PRESSURE BUILD: approx. 12 minutes
COOK: 15 minutes

1½ pounds (680 g) jumbo scallops, fresh or frozen
½ cup water
¼ cup unsalted butter, melted
2 garlic cloves, grated
Juice of ½ lemon, divided
Salt and freshly ground black pepper

1. Pour ½ cup water into the pot. Place the bottom rack in the pot and arrange the scallops.
2. Close lid and move slider to PRESSURE. Make sure the pressure release valve is in the SEAL position.
3. The temperature will default to HIGH, which is the correct setting. Select QUICK RELEASE. Set time to 0 minutes. Select START/STOP to begin cooking (the unit will build pressure for approx. 12 minutes before cooking begins).
4. Meanwhile, combine the butter, garlic, and half the lemon juice in a small bowl.
5. When cooking is complete and the pressure automatically releases, select START/STOP and move slider to AIR FRY/STOVETOP to unlock the lid, then carefully open it.
6. Remove the rack from pot. Drain any excess water and wipe the pot clean. Pat the scallops dry with a paper towel, season with salt and pepper to taste, and toss with the butter mixture. Reinsert the rack with scallops in the pot. Close lid and keep slider in the AIR FRY/STOVETOP position. Select AIR FRY, set temperature to 390°F and set time to 15 minutes. Select START/STOP to begin cooking.
7. When cooking is complete, transfer the scallops to a serving dish. Drizzle lightly with the remaining lemon juice. Serve immediately.

CHAPTER 4
VEGETABLES

Parmesan Broccoli / 23

Shishito Peppers with Dipping Sauce / 23

Ginger Lentil Stew / 24

Asparagus with Almond Slices / 24

Cheesy Barley Risotto with Mushroom / 25

Herbed Radishes / 25

Honey Beets and Red Onions / 26

Nutty Sprouts / 26

Authentic Mexican Street Corn / 26

Vegan Nuggets / 27

Tender Cabbage Wedges / 27

Crunchy Fried Okra / 28

Shakshouka with Kale / 28

Parmesan Broccoli

SERVES: 2

PREP: 10 minutes
TOTAL COOK TIME: 23 minutes
STEAM: approx. 8 minutes
COOK: 15 minutes

½ cup water, for steaming
cooking spray
1 tbsp. olive oil
10 ounces frozen broccoli
3 tbsps. balsamic vinegar
2 tbsps. Parmesan cheese, grated
⅛ tsp. cayenne pepper
Salt and black pepper, as required

1. Mix the broccoli, vinegar, olive oil, cayenne, salt, and black pepper in a bowl and toss to coat well.
2. Add ½ cup water to the pot. Spray the Cook & Crisp Basket with cooking spray, then place the basket in the pot. Add the broccoli to the basket. Close the lid and move slider to STEAMCRISP.
3. Select STEAM & CRISP, set temperature to 400°F, and set time to 15 minutes. Press START/STOP to begin cooking (PrE will display for approx. 8 minutes as the unit steams, then the timer will start counting down).
4. With 8 minutes remaining, open the lid and toss the broccoli with tongs. Close the lid to continue cooking.
5. When the cooking is complete, remove the basket from pot. Transfer the broccoli a bowl and top with Parmesan cheese to serve.

Shishito Peppers with Dipping Sauce

SERVES: 4

PREP TIME: 10 minutes
COOK TIME: 8 minutes

FOR THE DIPPING SAUCE:
1 cup sour cream
2 tbsps. fresh lemon juice
1 green onion (white and green parts), finely chopped
1 clove garlic, minced

FOR THE PEPPERS:
1 tbsp. vegetable oil
8 ounces (227 g) shishito peppers
1 tsp. toasted sesame oil
½ tsp. toasted sesame seeds
¼ to ½ tsp. red pepper flakes
Kosher salt and black pepper, to taste

1. In a small bowl, mix all the dipping sauce ingredients to combine well. Cover and refrigerate until serving time.
2. Close the lid and move slider to the AIR FRY/STOVETOP. Preheat the pot by selecting AIR FRY, setting temperature to 350°F, and setting time to 5 minutes. Select START/STOP to begin preheating.
3. While unit is preheating, stir the shishito peppers with the vegetable oil in a medium bowl.
4. Attach Cook & Crisp Basket with diffuser and spray with cooking spray, then add the peppers.
5. When the pot has preheated, place the basket in the pot. Close the lid and make sure the slider is still in the AIR FRY/STOVETOP.
6. Select AIR FRY, set temperature to 350°F, and set time to 8 minutes. Select START/STOP to begin cooking, tossing halfway through cooking.
7. When cooking is complete, remove the basket and transfer the peppers to a serving bowl. Pour in the sesame oil and toss to coat evenly. Sprinkle with salt and black pepper to taste. Place the red pepper flakes and sesame seeds and toss again.
8. Serve hot with the dipping sauce.

Ginger Lentil Stew

SERVES: 6

PREP TIME: 10 minutes
COOK TIME: 35 minutes

¼ cup vegetable oil
2 cups orange lentils, rinsed
1 cup fresh tomato, diced peeled
1 large sweet onion, chopped
3 garlic cloves, crushed
1 inch piece fresh ginger, grated
1 tsp. cumin seed, crushed

½ tsp. salt
1 tsp. cardamom seed, crushed
¼ tsp. ground cinnamon
½ tsp. cayenne pepper
1 tsp. coriander powder
1 tsp. turmeric

1. Close lid and move slider to AIR FRY/STOVETOP. Select SEAR/SAUTÉ and set to 3. Open lid and select START/STOP to begin preheating. Allow unit to preheat for 5 minutes.
2. After 5 minutes, stir the lentils with salt in the pot. Cover them with boiling water.
3. Let the lentils cook for about 22 minutes.
4. Once the time is up, drain the lentils and transfer into a mixing bowl and press it with a potato masher to mash it slightly.
5. Heat the vegetable oil in the pot. Add the onion with garlic and cook for 5 minutes.
6. Stir in the remaining ingredients. Cook for another 6 minutes. Add the lentils and heat them through.
7. Serve the lentil stew warm.

Asparagus with Almond Slices

SERVES: 3

PREP TIME: 15 minutes
COOK TIME: 8 minutes

cooking spray
2 tbsps. olive oil
1 pound asparagus
⅓ cup almonds, sliced
2 tbsps. balsamic vinegar
Salt and black pepper, to taste

1. Close the lid and move slider to the AIR FRY/STOVETOP. Preheat the pot by selecting BAKE/ROAST, setting temperature to 390°F, and setting time to 5 minutes. Select START/STOP to begin preheating.
2. While unit is preheating, mix the asparagus, olive oil, vinegar, salt, and black pepper in a bowl and toss to coat evenly.
3. Spray the Ninja Multi-Purpose Pan with cooking spray and arrange the asparagus. Sprinkle with the almond slices.
4. Place the pan on the bottom rack. When the pot has preheated, place the rack with pan in the pot. Close the lid and make sure the slider is still in the AIR FRY/STOVETOP.
5. Select BAKE/ROAST, set temperature to 390°F, and set time to 8 minutes. Select START/STOP to begin cooking, flipping halfway through cooking.
6. When cooking is complete, remove the rack with the pan. Serve hot.

Cheesy Barley Risotto with Mushroom

SERVES: 6 TO 8

PREP TIME: 12 minutes
COOK TIME: 7 hours

2¼ cups hulled barley, rinsed
1 (8-ounce / 227-g) package button mushrooms, chopped
1 onion, finely chopped
4 garlic cloves, minced
6 cups low-sodium vegetable broth
⅔ cup grated Parmesan cheese
½ tsp. dried marjoram leaves
⅛ tsp. freshly ground black pepper

1. Mix the barley, onion, garlic, mushrooms, broth, marjoram, and pepper in the pot.
2. Close the lid and move slider to AIR FRY/STOVETOP. Select SLOW COOK, set temperature to Lo, and set time to 7 hours. Press START/STOP to begin cooking, until the barley has absorbed most of the liquid and is soft, and the vegetables are tender.
3. When cooking is complete, toss in the Parmesan cheese and serve hot.

Herbed Radishes

SERVES: 2

PREP TIME: 5 minutes
COOK TIME: 10 minutes

cooking spray
2 tbsps. unsalted butter, melted
1 pound (454 g) radishes
½ tsp. garlic powder
½ tsp. dried parsley
¼ tsp. dried oregano

1. Prepare the radishes by cutting off their tops and bottoms and quartering them.
2. In a bowl, mix the butter, dried parsley, dried oregano, and garlic powder. Toss with the radishes to coat evenly.
3. Close the lid and move slider to the AIR FRY/STOVETOP. Preheat the pot by selecting AIR FRY, setting temperature to 390°F, and setting time to 5 minutes. Select START/STOP to begin preheating.
4. While unit is preheating, attach Cook & Crisp Basket with diffuser and spray with cooking spray, then arrange the radishes.
5. When the pot has preheated, place the basket in the pot. Close the lid and make sure the slider is still in the AIR FRY/STOVETOP.
6. Select AIR FRY, set temperature to 390°F, and set time to 10 minutes. Select START/STOP to begin cooking, tossing halfway through cooking.
7. When cooking is complete, remove the basket and let cool for 5 minutes, then serve warm.

Honey Beets and Red Onions

PREP TIME: 14 minutes	2 tbsps. melted coconut oil	⅓ cup lemon juice
COOK TIME: 6 hours	10 medium beets, peeled and sliced	⅓ cup honey
	3 red onions, chopped	4 garlic cloves, minced
	1 cup water	3 tbsps. cornstarch
		½ tsp. salt

1. Add the beets, onions, and garlic to the pot.
2. In a medium bowl, mix the coconut oil, honey, lemon juice, 1 cup water, cornstarch, and salt, until well combined. Add this mixture over the beets.
3. Close the lid and move slider to AIR FRY/STOVETOP. Select SLOW COOK, set temperature to Lo, and set time to 6 hours. Press START/STOP to begin cooking, until the beets are soft and the sauce has thickened.
4. When cooking is complete, let cool for about 5 minutes and serve warm.

Nutty Sprouts

PREP TIME: 15 minutes	4 pounds (1.8 kg) Brussels sprouts	¼ cup red wine vinegar
COOK TIME: 15 minutes	4 small red onions, cut into strips	2 tbsps. white sugar
	½ cup unsalted butter	Salt and pepper to taste
	½ cup coarsely chopped pistachios	

1. Arrange a steamer basket in a pan of the boiling water.
2. Place the Brussels sprouts in the steamer basket and cook, covered for about 8 to 10 minutes.
3. Close lid and move slider to AIR FRY/STOVETOP. Select SEAR/SAUTÉ and set to 3. Open lid and select START/STOP to begin preheating. Allow unit to preheat for 5 minutes.
4. After 5 minutes, add the butter to pot. Once it melts, add the onions and 3 tbsps. vinegar and sauté until the onions are browned.
5. Add the Brussels sprouts, white sugar and remaining vinegar and cook until the Brussels sprouts are lightly caramelized.
6. Season with the salt and pepper to taste and press START/STOP to turn off the cooker.
7. Serve garnished with pistachios.

Authentic Mexican Street Corn

PREP: 5 minutes	½ cup water, for steaming	2 tbsps. mayonnaise
TOTAL COOK TIME: 18 minutes	Cooking spray	2 tbsps. chopped fresh cilantro
STEAM: approx. 8 minutes	4 medium ears corn, husked	1 tbsp. fresh lime juice
COOK: 10 minutes	2 ounces (57 g) crumbled Cotija or Feta cheese	½ tsp. ancho chile powder
		¼ tsp. kosher salt

1. Spray the corn with cooking spray.
2. Add ½ cup water to the pot and place the basket in the pot. Add the corn to the basket. Close the lid and move slider to STEAMCRISP.
3. Select STEAM & CRISP, set temperature to 375°F, and set time to 10 minutes. Press START/STOP to begin cooking (PrE will display for approx. 8 minutes as the unit steams, then the timer will start counting down). Flip the corn halfway through cooking.
4. When the cooking is complete, remove the basket from pot and let cook for about 20 minutes. Cut the corn kernels off the cob.
5. In a large bowl, mix together lime juice, mayonnaise, ancho powder, and salt. Add the corn kernels and mix to combine well. Transfer to a serving dish and top with the Cotija cheese and chopped cilantro. Serve immediately.

Vegan Nuggets

PREP: 15 minutes
TOTAL COOK TIME: 21 minutes
STEAM: approx. 6 minutes
COOK: 15 minutes

½ cup water, for steaming
cooking spray
1 egg
1 cup panko breadcrumbs
1 cup all-purpose flour
1 zucchini, chopped roughly
½ of carrot, chopped roughly
1 tbsp. milk
1 tbsp. onion powder
1 tbsp. garlic powder
½ tbsp. mustard powder
Salt and black pepper, to taste

1. Put the zucchini, carrot, garlic powder, mustard powder, onion powder, salt and black pepper in a food processor and pulse until combined.
2. Place the flour in a shallow dish and whisk the eggs with milk in a second dish.
3. Add the breadcrumbs in a third shallow dish.
4. Coat the vegetable nuggets evenly in flour and dip in the egg mixture. Then roll into the breadcrumbs evenly.
5. Add ½ cup water to the pot. Spray the Cook & Crisp Basket with cooking spray, then place the basket in the pot. Add the nuggets to the basket, spreading it evenly across the basket. Close the lid and move slider to STEAM-CRISP.
6. Select STEAM & CRISP, set temperature to 350°F, and set time to 15 minutes. Press START/STOP to begin cooking (PrE will display for approx. 6 minutes as the unit steams, then the timer will start counting down). Flip the nuggets halfway through cooking.
7. When the cooking is complete, remove the basket from pot. Serve warm.

Tender Cabbage Wedges

PREP TIME: 15 minutes
COOK TIME: 2 hours

2 tbsps. unsalted butter
1 medium-sized savoy cabbage cut up into wedges
½ tsp. kosher salt

1. Add 12 cups of room-temperature water to the pot.
2. Close the lid and move slider to AIR FRY/STOVETOP, then use the dial to select SOUS VIDE. Select SOUS VIDE, set temperature to 180°F, and set time to 2 hours.
3. Press START/STOP to begin preheating.
4. In a Sous Vide bag, mix 1 tbsp. butter, salt, and cabbages.
5. When preheating is complete and "ADD FOOD" will show on the display.
6. Open the lid and place bag in the water using the water displacement method. When just the bag's seal is above the water line, finish closing the bag, making sure no water gets inside. Keep the bag's seal just above the water line. Close the lid.
7. When cooking is complete, remove the bag with cabbage, pat dry using kitchen towel.
8. In a medium-sized skillet, add the remaining tbsp. butter over medium heat.
9. Allow the butter to melt and place the cabbages. Sauté for 5-7 minutes until golden.
10. Serve and enjoy!

Crunchy Fried Okra

PREP TIME: 5 minutes COOK TIME: 10 minutes	Cooking spray 2 cups okra slices 2 large eggs, beaten 1 cup self-rising yellow cornmeal	1 tsp. Italian-style seasoning 1 tsp. paprika 1 tsp. salt ½ tsp. freshly ground black pepper

1. Close the lid and move slider to the AIR FRY/STOVETOP. Preheat the pot by selecting AIR FRY, setting temperature to 400°F, and setting time to 5 minutes. Select START/STOP to begin preheating.
2. While unit is preheating, whisk the cornmeal, Italian-style seasoning, paprika, salt, and black pepper in a shallow bowl, until blended. Place the beaten eggs in a second shallow bowl.
3. Add the okra to the beaten egg and stir to coat well. Put the egg and okra mixture to the cornmeal mixture and stir until coated evenly.
4. Attach Cook & Crisp Basket with diffuser and spray with cooking spray, then add the okra.
5. When the pot has preheated, place the basket in the pot. Close the lid and make sure the slider is still in the AIR FRY/STOVETOP.
6. Select AIR FRY, set temperature to 400°F, and set time to 10 minutes. Select START/STOP to begin cooking. Halfway through cooking, toss the okra and spray with cooking spray.
7. When cooking is complete, remove the basket and transfer the okra to a plate and serve hot.

Shakshouka with Kale

PREP: 10 minutes TOTAL COOK TIME: 32 minutes PRESSURE BUILD: approx. 10 minutes COOK: 22 minutes	6 large eggs 8 ounces (227 g) kale, tough stems and ribs removed, leaves finely chopped 3 tbsps. peanut oil or vegetable oil 1 medium yellow onion, diced 1 green bell pepper, ribbed, seeded, and diced 2 serrano chiles, ribbed, seeded, and diced 1 jalapeño, ribbed, seeded, and diced 1 bunch cilantro leaves, stems removed and leaves finely chopped 4 garlic cloves, minced Juice of ½ lemon 1 tbsp. ground cumin 1 tbsp. ground coriander 1 tsp. kosher salt

1. Close lid and move slider to AIR FRY/STOVETOP. Select SEAR/SAUTÉ and set to Hi5. Open lid and select START/STOP to begin preheating. Allow unit to preheat for 5 minutes.
2. After 5 minutes, add the oil, onion, garlic, bell pepper, chiles, and jalapeño to the pot and sauté for 6 minutes. Stir constantly.
3. Toss in the cumin and coriander and continue to cook for another 3 minutes.
4. Add the kale to the pot. Close lid and move slider to PRESSURE. Make sure the pressure release valve is in the SEAL position.
5. The temperature will default to HIGH, which is the correct setting. Select QUICK RELEASE. Set time to 5 minutes. Select START/STOP to begin cooking (the unit will build pressure for approx. 10 minutes before cooking begins).
6. When cooking is complete and the pressure automatically releases, select START/STOP and move slider to AIR FRY/STOVETOP to unlock the lid, then carefully open it.
7. Stir in the salt and lemon juice, then place the cilantro. Crack the eggs into a measuring cup. Carefully pour the eggs on top of the shakshuka.
8. Close lid and keep slider in the AIR FRY/STOVETOP position. Select AIR FRY, set temperature to 390°F and set time to 8 minutes. Select START/STOP to begin cooking.
9. When cooking is complete, sprinkle with feta and dill. Serve hot with pita or bread.

CHAPTER 5
LAMB

Garlicky Lamb Chops / 30

Herbed Lamb Shoulder / 30

Air Fried Lamb Ribs with Mint Yogurt / 31

Thyme Lamb Chops / 31

Roasted Lamb Leg / 32

Spiced Lamb Satay / 32

Cumin Lamb with Red Pepper / 33

Lamb Loin Chops with Mushroom Barley / 33

Thai Coconut Curry Lamb / 34

Italian Lamb Chops with Avocado Mayo / 34

Lime Lamb and Chiles / 35

Lamb Leg with Brussels Sprouts / 35

Spiced Lamb Steaks and Snap Pea Rice / 36

Garlicky Lamb Chops

PREP TIME: 20 minutes
COOK TIME: 14 minutes

cooking spray
¼ cup olive oil, divided
8 (4-ounce) lamb chops
1 bulb garlic, halved
1 tbsp. fresh oregano, chopped
1 tbsp. fresh thyme, chopped
Salt and black pepper, to taste

1. Rub the garlic halves with about 2 tbsps. olive oil.
2. Mix the remaining oil, herbs, salt and black pepper in a large bowl.
3. Coat the lamb chops with about 1 tbsp. herb mixture.
4. Close the lid and move slider to the AIR FRY/STOVETOP. Preheat the pot by selecting BAKE/ROAST, setting temperature to 390°F, and setting time to 5 minutes. Select START/STOP to begin preheating.
5. When the pot has preheated, spray the racks with cooking spray. Place the bottom rack in the pot and arrange 4 lamb chops and half the garlic. Place the top rack on the pot and put the another 4 lamb chops and half the garlic.
6. Close the lid and make sure the slider is still in the AIR FRY/STOVETOP.
7. Select BAKE/ROAST, set temperature to 390°F, and set time to 14 minutes. Select START/STOP to begin cooking.
8. When cooking is complete, remove the racks. Let cool for about 5 minutes and serve with herb mixture.

Herbed Lamb Shoulder

PREP TIME: 10 minutes
COOK TIME: 6 hours

2 tbsps. olive oil
2 pounds lamb shoulder, bones removed
2 rosemary sprigs
1 garlic clove
Salt and pepper to taste

1. Add 12 cups of room-temperature water to the pot.
2. Close the lid and move slider to AIR FRY/STOVETOP, then use the dial to select SOUS VIDE. Select SOUS VIDE, set temperature to 180°F, and set time to 6 hours.
3. Press START/STOP to begin preheating.
4. Season the lamb shoulder with salt and black pepper to taste.
5. Put the lamb shoulder into a Sous Vide bag, adding the rosemary sprigs, olive oil and garlic.
6. When preheating is complete and "ADD FOOD" will show on the display.
7. Open the lid and place bag in the water using the water displacement method. When just the bag's seal is above the water line, finish closing the bag, making sure no water gets inside. Keep the bag's seal just above the water line. Close the lid.
8. When cooking is complete, remove the bag with lamb from cooker.
9. In a large skillet, sear the lamb for 3 minutes on both sides.
10. Serve with boiled potatoes pouring the cooking juices over.

Air Fried Lamb Ribs with Mint Yogurt

SERVES: 4

PREP TIME: 5 minutes
COOK TIME: 18 minutes

cooking spray
1 pound (454 g) lamb ribs
1 cup Greek yogurt
¼ cup mint leaves, chopped
2 tbsps. mustard
1 tsp. rosemary, chopped
Salt and ground black pepper, to taste

1. Close the lid and move slider to the AIR FRY/STOVETOP. Preheat the pot by selecting AIR FRY, setting temperature to 350°F, and setting time to 5 minutes. Select START/STOP to begin preheating.
2. While unit is preheating, brush the lamb ribs with mustard, and season with rosemary, salt, and black pepper.
3. Attach Cook & Crisp Basket with diffuser and spray with cooking spray, then place the lamb ribs.
4. When the pot has preheated, place the basket in the pot. Close the lid and make sure the slider is still in the AIR FRY/STOVETOP.
5. Select AIR FRY, set temperature to 350°F, and set time to 18 minutes. Select START/STOP to begin cooking.
6. Meanwhile, combine the mint leaves and yogurt in a medium bowl.
7. When cooking is complete, remove the basket and transfer the lamb ribs to a plate. Serve hot with the mint yogurt.

Thyme Lamb Chops

SERVES: 4

PREP TIME: 10 minutes
COOK TIME: 2 hours

4 tbsps. olive oil, divided	2 tbsps. minced garlic
8 lamb chops	½ tbsp. lemon zest
4 sprigs fresh thyme	Salt and pepper, to taste

1. Add 12 cups of room-temperature water to the pot.
2. Close the lid and move slider to AIR FRY/STOVETOP, then use the dial to select SOUS VIDE. Select SOUS VIDE, set temperature to 145°F, and set time to 2 hours.
3. Press START/STOP to begin preheating.
4. Generously season the lamb chops with salt and black pepper.
5. In a Sous Vide bag, place the lamb chops along with 3 tbsps. olive oil, garlic, thyme sprigs, and lemon zest.
6. When preheating is complete and "ADD FOOD" will show on the display.
7. Open the lid and place bag in the water using the water displacement method. When just the bag's seal is above the water line, finish closing the bag, making sure no water gets inside. Keep the bag's seal just above the water line. Close the lid.
8. When cooking is complete, remove the bag with lamb from cooker.
9. Pat the lamb dry and keep aside.
10. In a skillet over medium heat, add 1 tbsp. oil. Sear the lamb chops for about 2 minutes per side, or use a torch to create a beautiful crust.
11. Serve hot.

Roasted Lamb Leg

SERVES: 4

PREP TIME: 15 minutes
COOK TIME: 40 minutes

cooking spray
1 tbsp. olive oil
2½ pounds half lamb leg roast, slits carved
2 garlic cloves, sliced into smaller slithers
1 tbsp. dried rosemary
Cracked Himalayan rock salt and cracked peppercorns, to taste

1. Insert the garlic slithers in the slits and brush with rosemary, olive oil, salt, and black pepper.
2. Close the lid and move slider to the AIR FRY/STOVETOP. Preheat the pot by selecting BAKE/ROAST, setting temperature to 400°F, and setting time to 5 minutes. Select START/STOP to begin pre-heating.
3. While unit is preheating, insert the garlic slithers in the slits and brush with rosemary, olive oil, salt, and black pepper.
4. Place the Foodi Smart Thermometer in the center of the thickest part of the meat.
5. When the pot has preheated, spray the bottom rack with cooking spray and arrange the lamb. Place the rack with lamb in the pot. Close the lid and make sure the slider is still in the AIR FRY/STOVETOP.
6. Select BAKE/ROAST, set temperature to 400°F, then select PRE-SET. Use the arrows to the right of the display to select LAMB. Press START/STOP to begin cooking.
7. When cooking is complete, remove the rack with lamb and serve hot.

Spiced Lamb Satay

SERVES: 2

PREP TIME: 5 minutes
COOK TIME: 10 minutes

Cooking spray
2 boneless lamb steaks
1 tsp. ginger
½ tsp. nutmeg
¼ tsp. cumin
Salt and ground black pepper, to taste

1. Mix the cumin, ginger, nutmeg, salt and pepper in a medium bowl.
2. Cut the lamb steaks into cubes and massage the spice mixture into each one.
3. Let marinate for about 10 minutes, then transfer onto metal skewers.
4. Close the lid and move slider to the AIR FRY/STOVETOP. Preheat the pot by selecting BAKE/ROAST, setting temperature to 375°F, and setting time to 5 minutes. Select START/STOP to begin pre-heating.
5. While unit is preheating, spray the Ninja Multi-Purpose Pan with cooking spray, then put the skewers.
6. Place the pan on the bottom rack. When the pot has preheated, place the rack with pan in the pot. Close the lid and make sure the slider is still in the AIR FRY/STOVETOP.
7. Select BAKE/ROAST, set temperature to 375°F, and set time to 10 minutes. Select START/STOP to begin cooking, flipping halfway through cooking.
8. When cooking is complete, remove the rack with the pan. Transfer the lamb to a serving plate and serve hot.

Cumin Lamb with Red Pepper

SERVES: 4

PREP TIME: 10 minutes **COOK TIME:** 5 minutes	2 tbsps. cooking oil 1 pound (454 g) boneless leg of lamb or shoulder, cut into 1-inch pieces 1 red bell pepper, cut into ½-inch pieces 1 medium onion, diced ½ cup cilantro, coarsely chopped 2 garlic cloves, crushed and chopped 2 tbsps. soy sauce 1 tbsp. cornstarch 1 tbsp. ginger, crushed and chopped 1 tbsp. ground cumin or cumin seeds 1 tbsp. rice wine 1 tbsp. rice vinegar ¼ tsp. kosher salt ½ tsp. ground black pepper

1. Close lid and move slider to AIR FRY/STOVETOP. Select SEAR/SAUTÉ and set to Hi5. Open lid and select START/STOP to begin preheating. Allow unit to preheat for 5 minutes.
2. After 5 minutes, heat the cooking oil in the pot until it shimmers.
3. Place the garlic, ginger and lamb and sear for about 1 minute.
4. Add the onion, cumin, salt and black pepper and sauté for about 1 minute.
5. Put the red bell pepper and sauté for about 1 minute.
6. Pour in the rice wine, rice vinegar, soy sauce and cornstarch and stir until a glaze is formed.
7. Top with the chopped cilantro and serve hot.

Lamb Loin Chops with Mushroom Barley

SERVES: 4

PREP: 20 minutes **TOTAL COOK TIME:** 28 minutes **STEAM:** approx. 15 minutes **COOK:** 13 minutes	**LEVEL 1 (BOTTOM OF POT)** 2 cups mushrooms, sliced 1 cup cooked hulled barley 2 cups water 2 cups cheesy vegetable sauce **LEVEL 2 (TOP RACK)** 1 tsp. olive oil 8 (3½-ounces) bone-in lamb loin chops, trimmed 3 garlic cloves, crushed 1 tbsp. fresh lemon juice Salt and black pepper, to taste **TOPPINGS:** Salsa Tzatziki

1. Place all Level 1 ingredients in the pot and stir until combined.
2. Mix the garlic, lemon juice, olive oil, salt, and black pepper in a large bowl.
3. Coat the lamb chops generously with the herb mixture. Place the top rack in the pot, then place the lamb chops on the rack. Close the lid and move slider to STEAMCRISP position.
4. Select STEAM & CRISP, set temperature to 375°F, and set time to 13 minutes. Press START/STOP to begin cooking (PrE will display for approx. 15 minutes as the unit steams, then the timer will start counting down).
5. When cooking is complete, remove the rack with the lamb chops. Stir the mushrooms and serve with lamb chops and desired toppings.

Thai Coconut Curry Lamb

PREP TIME: 8 minutes
COOK TIME: 5 minutes

1 pound (454 g) boneless lamb leg or shoulder, cut into 1-inch pieces
2 cups chopped bok choy
4 ounces (113 g) mushrooms, sliced
¼ cup canned coconut milk
1 medium onion, cut into 1-inch pieces
1 bird's eye chile, thinly sliced
2 garlic cloves, crushed and chopped
2 tbsps. coconut oil
1 tbsp. red Thai curry paste
1 tbsp. ginger, crushed and chopped
1 tbsp. brown sugar
1 tbsp. fish sauce
1 tbsp. cornstarch

1. In a small bowl, whisk together the coconut milk, brown sugar, curry paste, fish sauce and cornstarch. Keep aside.
2. Close lid and move slider to AIR FRY/STOVETOP. Select SEAR/SAUTÉ and set to Hi5. Open lid and select START/STOP to begin preheating. Allow unit to preheat for 5 minutes.
3. After 5 minutes, heat the coconut oil in the pot until it shimmers.
4. Put the garlic, ginger and lamb and sauté for about 1 minute.
5. Add the mushrooms, onion and bird's eye chile and sauté for about 1 minute.
6. Place the bok choy and sauté for about 30 seconds.
7. Stir in the curry paste mixture and toss until a glaze is formed.
8. Serve warm.

Italian Lamb Chops with Avocado Mayo

PREP: 5 minutes
TOTAL COOK TIME: 22 minutes
STEAM: approx. 6 minutes
COOK: 16 minutes

½ cup water, for steaming
2 lamb chops
2 avocados
½ cup mayonnaise
2 tsps. Italian herbs
1 tbsp. lemon juice

1. Season the lamb chops with the Italian herbs, then keep aside for about 5 minutes.
2. Add ½ cup water to the pot. Spray the Cook & Crisp Basket with cooking spray, then place the basket in the pot. Add the lamb chops to the basket. Close the lid and move slider to STEAMCRISP.
3. Select STEAM & CRISP, set temperature to 375°F, and set time to 16 minutes. Press START/STOP to begin cooking (PrE will display for approx. 6 minutes as the unit steams, then the timer will start counting down).
4. Meanwhile, halve the avocados and open to remove the pits. Scoop the flesh into a blender. Add the mayonnaise and lemon juice and pulse until a smooth consistency is achieved.
5. When the cooking is complete, remove the basket from pot. Carefully transfer the chops to a plate and serve hot with the avocado mayo.

Lime Lamb and Chiles

SERVES: 4	
PREP TIME: 11 minutes COOK TIME: 5 minutes	1 pound (454 g) lamb tenderloin, cut into 1-inch pieces, across the grain 1 medium onion, diced 2 or 3 Thai bird's eye chiles 4 scallions, cut into 1-inch pieces 2 garlic cloves, crushed and chopped Juice of 1 lime 2 tbsps. cooking oil 1 tbsp. hot sesame oil 1 tbsp. fish sauce 1 tbsp. soy sauce 1 tbsp. cornstarch 1 tbsp. brown sugar 1 tbsp. ginger, crushed and chopped

1. Whisk together the brown sugar, lime juice, sesame oil and cornstarch in a small bowl. Set aside.
2. Mix the soy sauce and fish sauce in a large bowl. Add the lamb pieces and massage for about 1 minute.
3. Close lid and move slider to AIR FRY/STOVETOP. Select SEAR/SAUTÉ and set to Hi5. Open lid and select START/STOP to begin preheating. Allow unit to preheat for 5 minutes.
4. After 5 minutes, heat the cooking oi in the pot until it shimmers.
5. Put the garlic, ginger and lamb and sear for about 1 minute.
6. Place the bird's eye chiles and onion and sauté for about 1 minute.
7. Pour in the lime juice mixture and stir until a glaze is formed.
8. Scatter with the scallions and serve warm.

Lamb Leg with Brussels Sprouts

SERVES: 6	
PREP TIME: 20 minutes COOK TIME: 35 minutes	cooking spray 2¼ pounds leg of lamb 3 tbsps. olive oil, divided 2 tbsps. honey 1 tbsp. fresh rosemary, minced 1 tbsp. fresh lemon thyme 1½ pounds Brussels sprouts, trimmed 1 garlic clove, minced Salt and ground black pepper, as required

1. Close the lid and move slider to the AIR FRY/STOVETOP. Preheat the pot by selecting BAKE/ROAST, setting temperature to 375°F, and setting time to 5 minutes. Select START/STOP to begin preheating.
2. While unit is preheating, make slits in the leg of lamb with a sharp knife.
3. Mix 2 tbsps. olive oil, herbs, garlic, salt, and black pepper in a bowl.
4. Coat the leg of lamb with oil mixture generously.
5. Spray the racks with cooking spray.
6. When the pot has preheated, place the bottom rack in the pot and arrange the leg lamb. Close the lid and make sure the slider is still in the AIR FRY/STOVETOP.
7. Select BAKE/ROAST, set temperature to 375°F, and set time to 35 minutes. Select START/STOP to begin cooking.
8. Meanwhile, coat the Brussels sprouts evenly with the remaining olive oil and honey
9. After 20 minutes, open the lid. Put the top rack on the pot and arrange the Brussels sprouts. Close the lid to continue cooking.
10. When cooking is complete, remove the rack with lamb, then the rack with Brussels sprouts. Let cool for 5 minutes and serve warm.

Spiced Lamb Steaks and Snap Pea Rice

PREP: 15 minutes
TOTAL COOK TIME: 27 minutes
STEAM: approx. 12 minutes
COOK: 15 minutes

LEVEL 1 (BOTTOM OF POT)
2 cups water
1 cup easy-cooked brown rice, rinsed
1 cup sugar snap peas
Salt, to taste
LEVEL 2 (TOP RACK)
½ onion, roughly chopped
1½ pounds boneless lamb sirloin steaks
5 garlic cloves, peeled
1 tbsp. fresh ginger, peeled
1 tsp. ground fennel
1 tsp. garam masala
½ tsp. cayenne pepper
¼ tsp. ground cinnamon
½ tsp. ground cumin
Salt and black pepper, to taste
TOPPINGS:
Mint sauce
Greek yogurt

1. In a blender, put the onion, garlic, ginger, and spices and pulse until smooth.
2. Coat the lamb steaks evenly with this mixture on both sides and refrigerate to marinate for about 24 hours.
3. Place all Level 1 ingredients in the pot and stir until combined.
4. Place the top rack in the pot, then place the lamb steaks on the rack. Close the lid and move slider to STEAM-CRISP position.
5. Select STEAM & CRISP, set temperature to 350°F, and set time to 15 minutes. Press START/STOP to begin cooking (PrE will display for approx. 12 minutes as the unit steams, then the timer will start counting down).
6. When cooking is complete, remove the rack with the lamb steaks. Stir the snap peas and serve with lamb steaks and desired toppings.

CHAPTER 6
BEEF

Beef Cheeseburgers / 38

Perfect Skirt Steak / 38

Sirloin Steak with Smashed Yukon

Potatoes / 39

Buttered Ribeye Steak / 39

Smoked Roast Beef / 40

Beef and Veggie Kebabs / 40

Classic Moroccan Beef Tagine / 41

Classic Brisket Chili Verde / 41

Corned Beef / 41

Sha Cha Beef with Sugar Snap / 42

Barbecue Brisket Burnt Ends / 42

Thai Beef Roast and Veggies / 43

Beef Steak and Mushroom Alfredo Rice / 43

Beef Cheeseburgers

SERVES: 2

PREP TIME: 15 minutes
COOK TIME: 12 minutes

cooking spray
½ pound ground beef
2 slices cheddar cheese
2 salad leaves
2 dinner rolls, cut into half
1 garlic clove, minced
2 tbsps. fresh cilantro, minced
Salt and black pepper, to taste

1. Mix the beef, garlic, cilantro, salt, and black pepper in a bowl.
2. Shape the beef mixture into 2 equal-sized patties.
3. Spray the bottom rack with cooking spray and arrange the patties. Place the rack with patties in the pot. Close the lid and move slider to the AIR FRY/STOVETOP.
4. Select BROIL, set temperature to 450°F, and time to 8 minutes. Press START/STOP to begin broiling.
5. With 1 minute remaining, open the lid and top each patty with 1 cheese slice. Close the lid to continue cooking.
6. When cooking is complete, place the dinner rolls in a serving platter and arrange salad leaf between each dinner roll. Top each with 1 patty and serve immediately.

Perfect Skirt Steak

SERVES: 4

PREP TIME: 15 minutes
COOK TIME: 10 minutes

cooking spray
¾ cup olive oil
2 (8-ounce) skirt steaks
1 cup fresh parsley leaves, chopped finely
3 garlic cloves, minced
3 tbsps. fresh mint leaves, chopped finely
3 tbsps. fresh oregano, chopped finely
3 tbsps. red wine vinegar
1 tbsp. ground cumin
2 tsps. smoked paprika
1 tsp. cayenne pepper
1 tsp. red pepper flakes, crushed
Salt and freshly ground black pepper, to taste

1. Season the steaks with salt and black pepper to taste.
2. Mix all the ingredients in a large bowl except the skirt steaks.
3. Put ¼ cup of the herb mixture and steaks in a resealable bag and shake well.
4. Refrigerate for 24 hours and reserve the remaining herb mixture.
5. Stand the steaks at room temperature for about 30 minutes.
6. Close the lid and move slider to the AIR FRY/STOVETOP. Preheat the pot by selecting BAKE/ROAST, setting temperature to 390°F, and setting time to 5 minutes. Select START/STOP to begin preheating.
7. While unit is preheating, spray the Ninja Multi-Purpose Pan with cooking spray, then add the steaks.
8. Place the pan on the bottom rack. When the pot has preheated, place the rack with pan in the pot. Close the lid and make sure the slider is still in the AIR FRY/STOVETOP.
9. Select BAKE/ROAST, set temperature to 390°F, and set time to 10 minutes. Select START/STOP to begin cooking, flipping the steaks halfway through cooking.
10. When cooking is complete, remove the rack with the pan and let cool for 5 minutes. Sprinkle with remaining herb mixture to serve.

Sirloin Steak with Smashed Yukon Potatoes

SERVES: 4

PREP TIME: 20 minutes
COOK TIME: 1 hour

Canola oil for searing	2 lbs. baby Yukon potatoes, cubed
4 tbsps. butter	¼ cup steak seasoning
4 sirloin steaks	Salt and pepper as needed

1. Add 12 cups of room-temperature water to the pot.
2. Close the lid and move slider to AIR FRY/STOVETOP, then use the dial to select SOUS VIDE. Select SOUS VIDE, set temperature to 145°F, and set time to 1 hour.
3. Press START/STOP to begin preheating.
4. Season the steaks with salt and pepper and place into a Sous Vide bag.
5. When preheating is complete and "ADD FOOD" will show on the display.
6. Open the lid and place bag in the water using the water displacement method. When just the bag's seal is above the water line, finish closing the bag, making sure no water gets inside. Keep the bag's seal just above the water line. Close the lid.
7. Meanwhile, cook the potatoes in boiling water for about 15 minutes.
8. Strain the potatoes into a large mixing bowl and add the butter. Mash with the back of your spoon until mixed well. Season with salt and pepper to taste.
9. When the steak is cooked, remove from the bag and pat it dry using a kitchen towel.
10. In a heavy bottomed pan, heat the oil over medium-heat. Sear the steaks for 1 minute per side.
11. Serve with the smashed potatoes.

Buttered Ribeye Steak

SERVES: 1

PREP TIME: 5 minutes
COOK TIME: 15 minutes

cooking spray
1 tbsp. peanut oil
1 (1-pound / 454-g) ribeye steak
½ tbsp. butter
½ tsp. thyme, chopped
Salt and ground black pepper, to taste

1. Close the lid and move slider to the AIR FRY/STOVETOP. Preheat the pot by selecting AIR FRY, setting temperature to 390°F, and setting time to 5 minutes. Select START/STOP to begin preheating.
2. While unit is preheating, season the steak with salt and pepper to taste. Coat the steak with peanut oil.
3. Place the Foodi Smart Thermometer in the center of the thickest part of the meat.
4. When the pot has preheated, spray the bottom rack with cooking spray and arrange the steak. Place the rack with steak in the pot. Close the lid and make sure the slider is still in the AIR FRY/STOVETOP.
5. Select AIR FRY, set temperature to 390°F, then select PRESET. Use the arrows to the right of the display to select BEEF. Press START/STOP to begin cooking.
6. After 10 minutes, open the lid and toss in the butter and thyme. Close the lid to continue cooking.
7. When cooking is complete, remove the rack with steak and let cool for 10 minutes. Serve warm.

Smoked Roast Beef

PREP TIME: 10 minutes
COOK TIME: 20 minutes

cooking spray
2 tbsps. extra-virgin olive oil
2 pounds (907 g) roast beef, at room temperature
2 jalapeño peppers, thinly sliced
1 tsp. smoked paprika
1 tsp. sea salt flakes
1 tsp. ground black pepper
Few dashes of liquid smoke

1. Close the lid and move slider to the AIR FRY/STOVETOP. Preheat the pot by selecting BAKE/ROAST, setting temperature to 390°F, and setting time to 5 minutes. Select START/STOP to begin preheating.
2. While unit is preheating, pat the beef dry with kitchen towels.
3. Massage the olive oil, salt, black pepper, and paprika into the meat. Cover with liquid smoke.
4. Place the Foodi Smart Thermometer in the center of the thickest part of the meat.
5. When the pot has preheated, spray the bottom rack with cooking spray and arrange the beef. Place the rack with beef in the pot. Close the lid and make sure the slider is still in the AIR FRY/STOVETOP.
6. Select BAKE/ROAST, set temperature to 390°F, then select PRE-SET. Use the arrows to the right of the display to select BEEF. Press START/STOP to begin cooking.
7. When cooking is complete, remove the rack with beef and let cool for 10 minutes. Serve topped with sliced jalapeños.

Beef and Veggie Kebabs

PREP TIME: 20 minutes
COOK TIME: 12 minutes

cooking spray
¼ cup olive oil
1 pound sirloin steak, cut into 1-inch chunks
1 large bell pepper, seeded and cut into 1-inch pieces
1 red onion, cut into 1-inch pieces
8 ounces baby Bella mushrooms, stems removed
¼ cup soy sauce
1 tbsp. garlic, minced
1 tsp. coconut sugar
½ tsp. ground cumin
Salt and black pepper, to taste

1. Mix the soy sauce, olive oil, garlic, coconut sugar, cumin, salt, and black pepper in a large bowl.
2. Coat the steak cubes generously with the marinade and refrigerate to marinate for 30 minutes.
3. Thread the steak cubes, bell pepper, mushrooms, and onion onto metal skewers. Spray with cooking spray.
4. Close the lid and move slider to the AIR FRY/STOVETOP. Preheat the pot by selecting BAKE/ROAST, setting temperature to 390°F, and setting time to 5 minutes. Select START/STOP to begin preheating.
5. When the pot has preheated, place the bottom rack in the pot and arrange the skewers. Close the lid and make sure the slider is still in the AIR FRY/STOVETOP.
6. Select BAKE/ROAST, set temperature to 390°F, and set time to 12 minutes. Select START/STOP to begin cooking, flipping halfway through cooking.
7. When cooking is complete, remove the rack with the skewers and serve hot.

Classic Moroccan Beef Tagine

SERVES: 8 TO 10

PREP TIME: 15 minutes COOK TIME: 4 hours	1 (3-pound / 1.4-kg) grass-fed beef sirloin roast, cut into 2-inch pieces 3 carrots, cut into chunks 2 onions, chopped 1 cup chopped dates	2 jalapeño peppers, minced 6 garlic cloves, minced 1 cup beef stock 2 tbsps. honey 2 tsps. ground cumin 1 tsp. ground turmeric

1. Add the carrots, onions, garlic, jalapeño peppers, and dates to the pot.
2. In a small bowl, mix the honey, beef stock, cumin, and turmeric until combined well. Pour the honey mixture into the pot.
3. Close the lid and move slider to AIR FRY/STOVETOP. Select SLOW COOK, set temperature to Hi, and set time to 4 hours. Press START/STOP to begin cooking, until the beef is soft.
4. When cooking is complete, let cool for 5 minutes and serve warm.

Classic Brisket Chili Verde

SERVES: 4

PREP: 10 minutes TOTAL COOK TIME: 28 minutes PRESSURE BUILD: approx. 10 minutes COOK: 18 minutes	1 pound (454 g) brisket, cooked 1 (19-ounce, 539 g) can green chile enchilada sauce 1 (4-ounce, 113 g) can fire-roasted diced green chiles ½ white onion, diced	1 jalapeño pepper, diced 1 tsp. garlic, minced Juice of 1 lime 1 tbsp. vegetable oil ½ tsp. ground chipotle pepper 1 tsp. seasoning salt

1. Close lid and move slider to AIR FRY/STOVETOP. Select SEAR/SAUTÉ and set to Hi5. Open lid and select START/STOP to begin preheating. Allow unit to preheat for 5 minutes.
2. After 5 minutes, add the oil, onion, jalapeño, and garlic to the pot and sauté for 3 minutes.
3. Add the brisket, enchilada sauce, green chiles, lime juice, salt, and chipotle powder. Mix well.
4. Close lid and move slider to PRESSURE. Make sure the pressure release valve is in the SEAL position.
5. The temperature will default to HIGH, which is the correct setting. Select QUICK RELEASE. Set time to 15 minutes. Select START/STOP to begin cooking (the unit will build pressure for approx. 10 minutes before cooking begins).
6. When cooking is complete and the pressure automatically releases, select START/STOP and move slider to AIR FRY/STOVETOP to unlock the lid, then carefully open it.
7. Serve hot.

Corned Beef

SERVES: 4

PREP TIME: 15 minutes COOK TIME: 15 minutes	1 tsp. vegetable oil 1 (12-ounce / 340-g) can corned beef ¼ green bell pepper, chopped ¼ onion, chopped ¼ cup water	2 tsps. tomato paste ¼ tsp. dried thyme ¼ tsp. crushed red pepper flakes Salt and pepper to taste

1. Close lid and move slider to AIR FRY/STOVETOP. Select SEAR/SAUTÉ and set to 3. Open lid and select START/STOP to begin preheating. Allow unit to preheat for 5 minutes.
2. After 5 minutes, heat the oil in the pot. Add the green bell pepper, onion, red pepper flakes and dried thyme and sauté for about 7 minutes.
3. Reduce the heat to Lo1 and toss in the tomato paste, salt and black pepper. Simmer for about 3 minutes.
4. Toss in the corned beef and ¼ cup water and simmer until all the liquid is absorbed. Serve hot.

Sha Cha Beef with Sugar Snap

SERVES: 4

PREP TIME: 9 minutes COOK TIME: 5 minutes	2 tbsps. cooking oil 1 pound (454 g) sirloin steak, sliced into ¼-inch strips 2 cups sugar snap or snow pea pods 1 medium onion, cut into 1-inch pieces 1 chile, cut into ¼-inch circles 4 scallions, cut into 1-inch pieces 2 cloves garlic, crushed and chopped ¼ cup sha cha 2 tbsps. Chinese rice wine 2 tbsps. soy sauce 1 tbsp. ginger, crushed and chopped

1. Close lid and move slider to AIR FRY/STOVETOP. Select SEAR/SAUTÉ and set to Hi5. Open lid and select START/STOP to begin preheating. Allow unit to preheat for 5 minutes.
2. After 5 minutes, heat the oil in the pot until it shimmers.
3. Add the garlic, ginger, onion, and steak strips and sauté for 1 minute.
4. Pour in the sha cha, rice wine, soy sauce, and chile and sauté for 1 minute.
5. Put the pea pods and scallions and cook for 1 minute.
6. Press START/STOP to turn off the cooker and serve hot.

Barbecue Brisket Burnt Ends

SERVES: 6

PREP: 5 minutes TOTAL COOK TIME: 2 hours 5 minutes PRESSURE BUILD: approx. 15 minutes COOK: 1 hour 50 minutes	3 pounds (1.4 kg) beef brisket, some (but not all) fat trimmed 1 cup water 2 cups barbecue sauce ¼ cup barbecue spice rub

1. Season the brisket liberally and evenly with the barbecue spice rub.
2. Pour 1 cup water into the pot and top with the brisket.
3. Place the Foodi Smart Thermometer in the center of the thickest part of the meat. Close lid and move slider to PRESSURE. Make sure the pressure release valve is in the SEAL position.
4. The temperature will default to HIGH, which is the correct setting. Select PRESET and choose the BEEF setting. Use the arrows to the left of the display to select SHRED. Select PRESSURE RELEASE and then select QUICK RELEASE. Press START/STOP to begin cooking.
5. When cooking is complete and the steam is released, select START/STOP and move slider to either STEAMCRISP or AIR FRY/STOVETOP to unlock the lid, then carefully open it.
6. Let cool slightly and cut the brisket into 2-inch chunks. Drain the cooking liquid from the pot. Place the brisket chunks in the pot. Add the barbecue sauce and stir to combine well.
7. Close lid and keep slider in the AIR FRY/STOVETOP position. Select AIR FRY, set temperature to 360°F, and set time to 20 minutes. Select START/STOP to begin cooking.
8. When cooking is complete, transfer the brisket chunks to a plate and serve immediately.

Thai Beef Roast and Veggies

SERVES: 10

PREP TIME: 14 minutes
COOK TIME: 9 hours

2½ pounds (1.1 kg) grass-fed beef sirloin roast, cut into 2-inch pieces
3 large carrots, shredded
3 large tomatoes, seeded and chopped
3 onions, chopped
1 small red chili pepper, minced
6 garlic cloves, minced
1 cup canned coconut milk
¾ cup peanut butter
½ cup beef stock
2 tbsps. grated fresh ginger root
3 tbsps. lime juice

1. Mix the carrots, tomatoes, onions, garlic, and ginger root in the pot.
2. In a medium bowl, mix the coconut milk, chili pepper, peanut butter, lime juice, and beef stock until blended well.
3. Top with the roast in the pot and pour the peanut sauce over all.
4. Close the lid and move slider to AIR FRY/STOVETOP. Select SLOW COOK, set temperature to Lo, and set time to 9 hours. Press START/STOP to begin cooking, until the beef is very soft.
5. When cooking is complete, serve immediately.

Beef Steak and Mushroom Alfredo Rice

SERVES: 4

PREP: 20 minutes
TOTAL COOK TIME: 27 minutes
STEAM: approx. 12 minutes
COOK: 15 minutes

LEVEL 1 (BOTTOM OF POT)
1 cup rice
2½ cups vegetable broth
¾ cup finely chopped onion
2 ounces (57 g) creamy mushroom Alfredo sauce
¼ cup coarsely chopped walnuts
2 tbsps. olive oil
2 garlic cloves, minced
1½ tbsps. fresh lemon juice
Salt and black pepper, to taste
LEVEL 2 (TOP RACK)
½ cup butter, melted
1 pound (454 g) beef steak
1 tsp. ground nutmeg
½ tsp. salt

1. Place all Level 1 ingredients in the pot and stir until combined.
2. Mix the beef steaks on all sides with melted butter, nutmeg, and salt.
3. Place the top rack in the pot, then place the beef steaks on the rack. Close the lid and move slider to STEAMCRISP position.
4. Select STEAM & CRISP, set temperature to 350°F, and set time to 15 minutes. Press START/STOP to begin cooking (PrE will display for approx. 12 minutes as the unit steams, then the timer will start counting down).
5. When cooking is complete, remove the rack with the beef steaks. Stir the onion and serve with beef steaks.

CHAPTER 7
PORK

Vietnamese Caramelized Pork with
Kimchi / 45

BBQ Flavored Pork Ribs / 45

Italian Sausage Meatballs / 46

Ketchup Pulled Pork / 46

Chinese Eggplant and Pork / 47

Mexican Pork Chops / 47

Crusted Pork Chops / 48

Lemony Pork Chop and Leeks / 48

Pork Chops and Carrot / 48

Pork Medallions / 49

Breaded Pork Chops and Cherry Tomato
Pasta / 49

Korean Style Pork Ribs / 50

Air Fried Baby Back Ribs / 50

Vietnamese Caramelized Pork with Kimchi

SERVES: 4

PREP TIME: 9 minutes
COOK TIME: 5 minutes

2 tbsps. coconut oil
1 pound (454 g) ground pork
1 medium onion, diced
½ cup chopped kimchi
¼ cup brown sugar
4 scallions, cut into ½-inch pieces
1 tbsp. fish sauce
2 garlic cloves, crushed and chopped
1 tbsp. ginger, crushed and chopped
1 tsp. ground black pepper

1. Close lid and move slider to AIR FRY/STOVETOP. Select SEAR/ SAUTÉ and set to Hi5. Open lid and select START/STOP to begin preheating. Allow unit to preheat for 5 minutes.
2. After 5 minutes, heat the coconut oil in the pot until it shimmers.
3. Add the pork, garlic, ginger, and onion and sear for about 2 minutes.
4. Put the fish sauce, black pepper and brown sugar and sauté for about 1 minute.
5. Place the kimchi and sauté for about 30 seconds.
6. Press START/STOP to turn off the cooker. Top with the scallions and serve hot.

BBQ Flavored Pork Ribs

SERVES: 6

PREP TIME: 10 minutes
COOK TIME: 15 minutes

cooking spray
1¾ pounds pork ribs
¾ cup BBQ sauce
¼ cup honey, divided
2 tbsps. tomato ketchup

1 tbsp. soy sauce
1 tbsp. Worcestershire sauce
½ tsp. garlic powder
Freshly ground white pepper, to taste

1. Mix 3 tbsps. honey and remaining ingredients in a large bowl except the pork ribs.
2. Coat the ribs with marinade generously and cover to refrigerate for about 30 minutes.
3. Close the lid and move slider to the AIR FRY/STOVETOP. Preheat the pot by selecting BAKE/ROAST, setting temperature to 375°F, and setting time to 5 minutes. Select START/STOP to begin pre- heating.
4. When the pot has preheated, place the bottom rack in the pot and arrange the ribs. Spray with cooking spray. Close the lid and make sure the slider is still in the AIR FRY/STOVETOP.
5. Select BAKE/ROAST, set temperature to 375°F, and set time to 15 minutes. Select START/STOP to begin cooking, flipping halfway through cooking.
6. When cooking is complete, remove the rack with the ribs and let cool for 5 minutes. Coat evenly with remaining honey and serve hot.

Italian Sausage Meatballs

SERVES: 4

PREP: 15 minutes
TOTAL COOK TIME: 16 minutes
STEAM: approx. 6 minutes
COOK: 10 minutes

½ cup water, for steaming
3½ ounces sausage, casing removed
½ medium onion, minced finely
3 tbsps. Italian breadcrumbs
1 tsp. fresh sage, chopped finely
½ tsp. garlic, minced
Salt and black pepper, to taste

1. Mix all the ingredients in a medium bowl until well combined.
2. Shape the mixture into equal-sized balls.
3. Add ½ cup water to the pot. Place the Cook & Crisp Basket in the pot and arrange the meatballs. Close the lid and move slider to STEAMCRISP.
4. Select STEAM & CRISP, set temperature to 375°F, and set time to 10 minutes. Press START/STOP to begin cooking (PrE will display for approx. 6 minutes as the unit steams, then the timer will start counting down).
5. With 5 minutes remaining, open the lid and flip the meatballs with tongs. Close the lid to continue cooking.
6. When the cooking is complete, remove the basket from pot and serve hot.

Ketchup Pulled Pork

SERVES: 6

PREP TIME: 10 minutes
COOK TIME: 24 hours

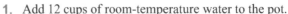

2 lbs. pork shoulder, trimmed
1 tbsp. ketchup
4 tbsps. Dijon mustard
2 tbsps. maple syrup
2 tbsps. soy sauce

1. Add 12 cups of room-temperature water to the pot.
2. Close the lid and move slider to AIR FRY/STOVETOP, then use the dial to select SOUS VIDE. Select SOUS VIDE, set temperature to 165°F, and set time to 24 hours.
3. Press START/STOP to begin preheating.
4. In a bowl, combine the ketchup, maple syrup, mustard, and soy sauce.
5. Wrap the pork shoulder with prepared sauce in plastic wrap, then put into Sous Vide bag.
6. When preheating is complete and "ADD FOOD" will show on the display.
7. Open the lid and place bag in the water using the water displacement method. When just the bag's seal is above the water line, finish closing the bag, making sure no water gets inside. Keep the bag's seal just above the water line. Close the lid.
8. When cooking is complete, open the bag and remove pork.
9. Strain the cooking juices into a saucepan. Torch the pork to create a crust.
10. Simmer the cooking juices in the saucepan until thickened.
11. Pull pork and serve with thickened sauce.

Chinese Eggplant and Pork

SERVES: 5

PREP TIME: 11 minutes
COOK TIME: 5 minutes

2 tbsps. cooking oil
1 pound (454 g) ground pork
1 small eggplant, diced into ½-inch cubes
¼ cup sriracha
4 scallions, cut into 1-inch pieces
2 garlic cloves, crushed and chopped
2 chiles, cut into ¼-inch circles (no need to core or seed)
2 tbsps. hoisin sauce
1 tbsp. ginger, crushed and chopped

1. Close lid and move slider to AIR FRY/STOVETOP. Select SEAR/SAUTÉ and set to Hi5. Open lid and select START/STOP to begin preheating. Allow unit to preheat for 5 minutes.
2. After 5 minutes, heat the cooking oil in the pot until it shimmers.
3. Add the chopped garlic, ginger and eggplant and sauté for about 1 minute.
4. Put the pork and sauté for about 2 minutes.
5. Stir in the sriracha, chiles and hoisin sauce and cook for about 1 minute.
6. Press START/STOP to turn off the cooker. Top with the scallions and serve hot.

Mexican Pork Chops

SERVES: 2

PREP TIME: 5 minutes
COOK TIME: 17 minutes

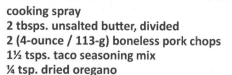

cooking spray
2 tbsps. unsalted butter, divided
2 (4-ounce / 113-g) boneless pork chops
1½ tsps. taco seasoning mix
¼ tsp. dried oregano

1. Close the lid and move slider to the AIR FRY/STOVETOP. Preheat the pot by selecting BAKE/ROAST, setting temperature to 375°F, and setting time to 5 minutes. Select START/STOP to begin preheating.
2. While unit is preheating, combine the dried oregano and taco seasoning in a small bowl and rub the taco mixture into the pork chops. Brush the chops with 1 tbsp. butter.
3. Spray the bottom rack with cooking spray and arrange the chops.
4. When the pot has preheated, place the rack with chops in the pot. Close the lid and make sure the slider is still in the AIR FRY/STOVETOP.
5. Select BAKE/ROAST, set temperature to 375°F, and set time to 17 minutes. Select START/STOP to begin cooking, flipping halfway through cooking.
6. When cooking is complete, remove the rack with the chops and let cool for 5 minutes. Serve with a garnish of remaining butter.

Crusted Pork Chops

PREP TIME: 10 minutes COOK TIME: 18 minutes	Cooking spray 4 to 6 thick boneless pork chops 2 beaten eggs 1 cup pork rind crumbs 3 tbsps. grated Parmesan cheese	1 tsp. smoked paprika ½ tsp. onion powder ½ tsp. salt ¼ tsp. black pepper ¼ tsp. chili powder

1. Rub the black pepper and salt on both sides of pork chops.
2. In a food processor, pulse the pork rinds into crumbs. Mix the crumbs with chili powder, onion powder, and paprika in a bowl. Beat the eggs in another bowl. Dip the pork chops into eggs, then into pork rind crumb mixture.
3. Close the lid and move slider to the AIR FRY/STOVETOP. Preheat the pot by selecting AIR FRY, setting temperature to 375°F, and setting time to 5 minutes. Select START/STOP to begin preheating.
4. While unit is preheating, attach Cook & Crisp Basket with diffuser and spray with cooking spray, then add the pork chops.
5. When the pot has preheated, place the basket in the pot. Close the lid and make sure the slider is still in the AIR FRY/STOVETOP.
6. Select AIR FRY, set temperature to 375°F, and set time to 18 minutes. Select START/STOP to begin cooking.
7. When cooking is complete, remove the basket and serve garnished with the Parmesan cheese.

Lemony Pork Chop and Leeks

PREP TIME: 18 minutes COOK TIME: 7 hours	8 (5-ounce / 142-g) bone-in pork loin chops 2 red bell peppers, stemmed, seeded, and chopped 2 leeks, chopped 8 garlic cloves, sliced 1 cup chicken stock ⅓ cup lemon juice 1 tsp. dried thyme leaves ½ tsp. salt

1. Add the garlic, leeks, and red bell peppers to the pot. Top with the pork chops.
2. In a small bowl, mix the thyme, lemon juice, chicken stock, and salt. Pour the lemon mixture over the pork.
3. Close the lid and move slider to AIR FRY/STOVETOP. Select SLOW COOK, set temperature to Lo, and set time to 7 hours. Press START/STOP to begin cooking, until the chops register at least 145°F on a food thermometer.
4. When cooking is complete, let cool for about 5 minutes and serve warm.

Pork Chops and Carrot

PREP TIME: 20 minutes COOK TIME: 4 hours	8 (5-ounce / 142-g) pork chops 4 large carrots, peeled and cut into chunks 2 onions, chopped 3 garlic cloves, minced ½ cup chicken stock	3 tbsps. honey 3 tbsps. grated fresh ginger root ½ tsp. ground ginger ½ tsp. salt ⅛ tsp. freshly ground black pepper

1. Mix the onions, garlic, and carrots in the pot and top with the pork chops.
2. Mix the ginger root, honey, chicken stock, ginger, salt, and black pepper in a small bowl. Pour the mixture into the pot.
3. Close the lid and move slider to AIR FRY/STOVETOP. Select SLOW COOK, set temperature to Hi, and set time to 4 hours. Press START/STOP to begin cooking, until the pork is very soft.
4. When cooking is complete, let cool for 5 minutes and serve warm.

Pork Medallions

SERVES: 4

PREP TIME: 10 minutes
COOK TIME: 1 hour 6 minutes

1 tbsp. olive oil
1¾ lbs. pork tenderloin
¼ cup chopped fresh parsley
1 tsp. ground cumin
1 pinch salt
1 pinch black pepper

1. Add 12 cups of room-temperature water to the pot.
2. Close the lid and move slider to AIR FRY/STOVETOP, then use the dial to select SOUS VIDE. Select SOUS VIDE, set temperature to 185°F, and set time to 1 hour.
3. Press START/STOP to begin preheating.
4. Cut the pork tenderloin in medallions. Season with salt, black pepper, and cumin. Place the seasoned pork into Sous Vide bag and add the parsley.
5. When preheating is complete and "ADD FOOD" will show on the display.
6. Open the lid and place bag in the water using the water displacement method. When just the bag's seal is above the water line, finish closing the bag, making sure no water gets inside. Keep the bag's seal just above the water line. Close the lid.
7. When cooking is complete, remove the bag with medallions from cooker.
8. In a large skillet, heat olive oil and sear for 3 minutes on both sides. Serve warm.

Breaded Pork Chops and Cherry Tomato Pasta

SERVES: 2

PREP: 15 minutes
TOTAL COOK TIME: 30 minutes
STEAM: approx. 15 minutes
COOK: 15 minutes

LEVEL 1 (BOTTOM OF POT)	LEVEL 3 (TOP RACK)
8 ounces plain pasta	1 tbsp. vegetable oil
½ cup tomato sauce	2 (6-ounces) pork chops
2 cups water	1 egg
LEVEL 2 (BOTTOM RACK)	4 ounces breadcrumbs
½ cup fresh zucchini, chopped	¼ cup plain flour
½ cup cherry tomatoes	Salt and black pepper, to taste
A pinch of salt and black pepper	TOPPINGS:
	Fresh basil
	Greek yogurt

1. Place all Level 1 ingredients in the pot and stir until evenly combined.
2. Place all Level 2 ingredients in a large bowl and stir until combined. Cover the bottom rack with aluminum foil, then place the rack in the pot. Place the vegetables on top of the foil.
3. Season the pork chops with salt and black pepper to taste. Add the flour in a shallow bowl and whisk an egg in a second bowl. Mix the breadcrumbs and vegetable oil in a third bowl.
4. Coat the pork chops with flour, dip into egg and then dredge into the breadcrumb mixture.
5. Place the top rack in the pot. Place the pork chops on the top rack. Close the lid and move slider to STEAMCRISP.
6. Select STEAM & CRISP, set temperature to 375°F, and set time to 15 minutes. Press START/STOP to begin cooking (PrE will display for approx. 15 minutes as the unit steams, then the timer will start counting down).
7. When cooking is complete, remove the rack with the pork chops, then the rack with the vegetables. Stir the pasta and serve warm with pork chops, vegetables and desired toppings.

Korean Style Pork Ribs

PREP: 10 minutes TOTAL COOK TIME: 40 minutes PRESSURE BUILD: approx. 15 minutes COOK: 25 minutes	1 (3-pound, 1.4 kg) rack baby back ribs, cut into quarters 1 small onion, minced ½ cup water ½ cup soy sauce ¼ cup honey 8 garlic cloves, minced 2 tbsps. sesame oil 2 tbsps. rice vinegar 1 tbsp. grated fresh ginger 1 tbsp. cayenne pepper Sesame seeds, for garnish

1. Combine the sesame oil, soy sauce, rice vinegar, cayenne pepper, garlic, ginger, and onion in a mixing bowl. Pour the mixture over the pork ribs, cover, and refrigerate for about 30 minutes.
2. Place the ribs and ½ cup water in the pot, reserving the remaining marinade.
3. Close lid and move slider to PRESSURE. Make sure the pressure release valve is in the SEAL position.
4. The temperature will default to HIGH, which is the correct setting. Select QUICK RELEASE. Set time to 10 minutes. Select START/STOP to begin cooking (the unit will build pressure for approx. 15 minutes before cooking begins).
5. When cooking is complete and the pressure automatically releases, select START/STOP and move slider to AIR FRY/STOVETOP to unlock the lid, then carefully open it.
6. Pour the remaining marinade over the ribs and toss well.
7. Close lid and keep slider in the AIR FRY/STOVETOP position. Select AIR FRY, set temperature to 400°F and set time to 15 minutes. Select START/STOP to begin cooking.
8. After 10 minutes, liberally brush the ribs with the honey and continue cooking for 5 minutes.
9. Once cooked, remove the ribs from pot. Cut them into individual ribs. Sprinkle with the sesame seeds and serve hot.

Air Fried Baby Back Ribs

PREP TIME: 5 minutes COOK TIME: 25 minutes	cooking spray 2 baby back ribs 2 tsps. red pepper flakes ¾ tsp. ground ginger 3 cloves minced garlic Salt and ground black pepper, to taste

1. Close the lid and move slider to the AIR FRY/STOVETOP. Preheat the pot by selecting AIR FRY, setting temperature to 350°F, and setting time to 5 minutes. Select START/STOP to begin preheating.
2. While unit is preheating, mix the garlic, ginger, red pepper flakes, salt and black pepper in a bowl, making sure to mix well. Massage the mixture into the baby back ribs.
3. Attach Cook & Crisp Basket with diffuser and spray with cooking spray, then add the baby back ribs.
4. When the pot has preheated, place the basket in the pot. Close the lid and make sure the slider is still in the AIR FRY/STOVETOP.
5. Select AIR FRY, set temperature to 350°F, and set time to 25 minutes. Select START/STOP to begin cooking, flipping halfway through cooking.
6. When cooking is complete, transfer the ribs to a serving dish and serve hot.

CHAPTER 8
POULTRY

Chicken Nuggets / 52

Simple Crispy Chicken Wings / 52

Mediterranean Chicken with Sun-dried
Tomato / 53

Confit Duck Leg with Cranberry Sauce / 53

Breaded Chicken Cutlets / 54

Garlic Soy Chicken Thighs / 54

Little Bay Yellow Curry / 55

Jerk Chicken Thigh / 55

Chili Chicken Dish / 55

Spiced Turkey Tenderloin / 56

Cheese Chicken Breasts and Tomatoes / 56

Kadai Chicken with Carrot / 57

Yummy Stuffed Chicken Breast with
Fettuccine / 57

Chicken Nuggets

SERVES: 4

PREP: 15 minutes
TOTAL COOK TIME: 25 minutes
STEAM: approx. 8 minutes
COOK: 15 minutes

½ cup water, for steaming
20-ounce chicken breast, cut into chunks
1 egg
1 cup panko breadcrumbs
1 cup all-purpose flour

2 tbsps. milk
½ tbsp. mustard powder
1 tbsp. onion powder
1 tbsp. garlic powder
Salt and black pepper, to taste

1. Put the chicken, garlic powder, onion powder, mustard powder, salt and black pepper in a food processor and pulse until combined.
2. Add the flour in a shallow dish and whisk the eggs with milk in a second dish.
3. Place the breadcrumbs in a third shallow dish.
4. Shape the chicken mixture into nuggets. Coat the nuggets evenly in flour and dip in the egg mixture. Roll into the breadcrumbs evenly.
5. Add ½ cup water to the pot. Spray the racks with cooking spray. Place the bottom rack in the pot and arrange half of nuggets. Place the top rack on the pot and put the remaining half of nuggets. Close the lid and move slider to STEAMCRISP.
6. Select STEAM & CRISP, set temperature to 375°F, and set time to 15 minutes. Press START/STOP to begin cooking (PrE will display for approx. 8 minutes as the unit steams, then the timer will start counting down).
7. With 7 minutes remaining, open the lid and flip the nuggets. Close the lid to continue cooking.
8. When the cooking is complete, remove the racks with nuggets from pot. Serve hot.

Simple Crispy Chicken Wings

SERVES: 4

PREP: 5 minutes
TOTAL COOK TIME: 33 minutes
PRESSURE BUILD: approx. 12 minutes
COOK: 21 minutes

1 tbsp. olive oil
1¼ pounds (567 g) chicken wings
1 cup water
¼ cup hot sauce

1 tbsp. butter
1 tsp. salt
½ tsp. black pepper

1. Place the chicken wings and 1 cup water into the pot.
2. Close lid and move slider to PRESSURE. Make sure the pressure release valve is in the SEAL position.
3. The temperature will default to HIGH, which is the correct setting. Select QUICK RELEASE. Set time to 5 minutes. Select START/STOP to begin cooking (the unit will build pressure for approx. 12 minutes before cooking begins).
4. When cooking is complete and the pressure automatically releases, select START/STOP and move slider to AIR FRY/STOVETOP to unlock the lid, then carefully open it.
5. Pat the chicken wings dry with a paper towel. Drizzle the chicken wings with the olive oil, salt, and pepper. Drain any remaining water from the pot and wipe it clean.
6. Close lid and keep slider in the AIR FRY/STOVETOP position. Select AIR FRY, set temperature to 400°F, and set time to 16 minutes. Select START/STOP to begin cooking, flipping halfway through cooking.
7. Meanwhile, mix the butter and hot sauce in a large bowl. Stir well.
8. When cooking is complete, transfer the wings to the bowl with the sauce and toss to coat the wings in sauce. Serve immediately.

Mediterranean Chicken with Sun-dried Tomato

SERVES: 2

PREP TIME: 10 minutes
COOK TIME: 1½ hours

1 tbsp. olive oil
2 chicken breast fillets
½ cup sun-dried tomatoes, packed in oil

2 tbsps. oil, from the sun-dried tomatoes
1 sprig basil
Salt and black pepper, to taste

1. Add 12 cups of room-temperature water to the pot.
2. Close the lid and move slider to AIR FRY/STOVETOP, then use the dial to select SOUS VIDE. Select SOUS VIDE, set temperature to 165°F, and set time to 1½ hours.
3. Press START/STOP to begin preheating.
4. Season the chicken with salt and pepper to taste.
5. Heat the olive oil in a large skillet. Add the chicken breasts and sear for 1 minute per side.
6. Transfer the chicken into a Sous Vide bag, and add the remaining ingredients.
7. When preheating is complete and "ADD FOOD" will show on the display.
8. Open the lid and place bag in the water using the water displacement method. When just the bag's seal is above the water line, finish closing the bag, making sure no water gets inside. Keep the bag's seal just above the water line. Close the lid.
9. When cooking is complete, remove the bag with chicken breasts from cooker.
10. Open the bag and transfer the chicken to a warmed plate. Serve immediately.

Confit Duck Leg with Cranberry Sauce

SERVES: 2

PREP TIME: 10-12 hours
COOK TIME: 4 hours

2 duck legs
6 tbsps. duck fat
2 big bay leaves, crushed

1 tbsp. dried thyme
Salt and pepper to taste
Cranberry sauce for serving

1. Mix the bay leaves with salt, black pepper and thyme, and season the duck legs with the mixture. Refrigerate overnight.
2. In the morning, rinse the legs with cold water and gently put them into the Sous Vide bag. Then add 4 tbsps. duck fat.
3. Add 12 cups of room-temperature water to the pot.
4. Close the lid and move slider to AIR FRY/STOVETOP, then use the dial to select SOUS VIDE. Select SOUS VIDE, set temperature to 165°F, and set time to 4 hours.
5. Press START/STOP to begin preheating.
6. When preheating is complete and "ADD FOOD" will show on the display.
7. Open the lid and place bag in the water using the water displacement method. When just the bag's seal is above the water line, finish closing the bag, making sure no water gets inside. Keep the bag's seal just above the water line. Close the lid.
8. When cooking is complete, remove the bag with duck legs from cooker.
9. Before serving, roast the legs in 2 remaining tbsps. duck fat until crispy.
10. Serve hot with cranberry sauce.

Breaded Chicken Cutlets

SERVES: 4

PREP TIME: 15 minutes
COOK TIME: 20 minutes

cooking spray
4 (6-ounces) (¼-inch thick) skin-less, boneless chicken cutlets
2 large eggs
1½ cups panko breadcrumbs
¾ cup all-purpose flour
¼ cup Parmesan cheese, grated
1 tbsp. mustard powder
Salt and black pepper, to taste

1. Close the lid and move slider to the AIR FRY/STOVETOP. Preheat the pot by selecting AIR FRY, setting temperature to 390°F, and setting time to 5 minutes. Select START/STOP to begin preheating.
2. While unit is preheating, place the flour in a shallow bowl and whisk the eggs in a second bowl. Mix the breadcrumbs, mustard powder, cheese, salt, and black pepper in a third bowl.
3. Season the chicken cutlets with salt and black pepper and coat the chicken with flour. Dip the chicken into whisked eggs and finally dredge into the breadcrumb mixture.
4. Attach Cook & Crisp Basket with diffuser and spray with cooking spray, then add the breaded chicken cutlets.
5. When the pot has preheated, place the basket in the pot. Close the lid and make sure the slider is still in the AIR FRY/STOVETOP.
6. Select AIR FRY, set temperature to 390°F, and set time to 20 minutes. Select START/STOP to begin cooking, flipping halfway through cooking.
7. When cooking is complete, remove the basket and transfer the chicken cutlets a platter. Serve immediately.

Garlic Soy Chicken Thighs

SERVES: 2

PREP TIME: 10 minutes
COOK TIME: 25 minutes

cooking spray
2 bone-in, skin-on chicken thighs (7 to 8 ounces / 198 to 227 g each)
4 garlic cloves, smashed and peeled
2 tbsps. reduced-sodium soy sauce
2 tbsps. chicken stock
1½ tbsps. sugar
2 large scallions, cut into 2- to 3-inch batons, plus more, thinly sliced, for garnish

1. Close the lid and move slider to the AIR FRY/STOVETOP. Preheat the pot by selecting BAKE/ROAST, setting temperature to 390°F, and setting time to 5 minutes. Select START/STOP to begin pre-heating.
2. While unit is preheating, combine the chicken stock, soy sauce, and sugar in a baking pan and stir until the sugar dissolves. Place the garlic cloves, scallions, and chicken thighs, turning the thighs to coat them evenly in the marinade, then resting them skin-side up.
3. When the pot has preheated, place the bottom rack in the pot and arrange the chicken thighs. Close the lid and make sure the slider is still in the AIR FRY/STOVETOP.
4. Select BAKE/ROAST, set temperature to 390°F, and set time to 25 minutes. Select START/STOP to begin cooking, flipping twice during cooking. Cook until the thighs are cooked through and the marinade is reduced to a sticky glaze over the chicken.
5. When cooking is complete, remove the rack with the chicken thighs and let cool for 5 minutes. Serve warm with any remaining glaze spooned over top and scattered with more sliced scallions.

Little Bay Yellow Curry

SERVES: 4

PREP TIME: 15 minutes
COOK TIME: 45 minutes
	2 tbsps. vegetable oil
	1 (14-ounce / 397-g) can unsweetened
	  coconut milk
	1 pound (454 g) skinless, boneless
	  chicken breast halves, chopped
	1 small head cauliflower, chopped
		⅓ cup chicken stock
		1 white onion, chopped
		1 tsp. garlic salt
		2 cloves garlic, crushed
		2½ tbsps. yellow curry powder
		Salt and pepper to taste

1. Close lid and move slider to AIR FRY/STOVETOP. Select SEAR/SAUTÉ and set to 3. Open lid and select START/STOP to begin preheating. Allow unit to preheat for 5 minutes.
2. After 5 minutes, heat the oil in the pot. Add the onion and garlic and sauté until tender.
3. Toss in the chicken and sear for about 10 minutes.
4. Stir in the cauliflower, coconut milk, chicken stock, garlic salt, curry powder, salt and pepper.
5. Reduce the heat to Lo1 and simmer for about 30 minutes, stirring occasionally. Serve hot.

Jerk Chicken Thigh

SERVES: 6

PREP TIME: 13 minutes COOK TIME: 4 hours	10 (4-ounce / 113-g) boneless, skin- less chicken thighs 3 onions, chopped ½ cup freshly squeezed orange juice 6 garlic cloves, minced 3 tbsps. grated fresh ginger root	2 tbsps. honey 1 tbsp. chili powder 1 tsp. ground red chili ¼ tsp. ground allspice ½ tsp. ground cloves

1. Cut slashes across the chicken thighs so the flavorings can permeate.
2. Mix the honey, ginger, ground chili, chili powder, cloves, and allspice in a small bowl. Gently rub this spice mixture into the chicken. Allow the chicken to sit while you make the vegetables.
3. Place the onions and garlic to the pot. Then top with the chicken and pour in the orange juice over all.
4. Close the lid and move slider to AIR FRY/STOVETOP. Select SLOW COOK, set temperature to Hi, and set time to 4 hours. Press START/STOP to begin cooking, until a food thermometer registers 165°F.
5. When cooking is complete, let cool for about 5 minutes and serve warm.

Chili Chicken Dish

SERVES: 4

PREP TIME: 6 minutes COOK TIME: 7 hours	8 (6-ounce / 170-g) boneless, skinless chicken breasts 2 (8-ounce / 227-g) BPA-free cans no-salt-added tomato sauce 2 onions, minced 8 garlic cloves, minced ⅓ cup mustard 3 tbsps. molasses 2 tbsps. lemon juice 1 tbsp. chili powder 2 tsps. paprika ¼ tsp. cayenne pepper

1. Mix the onions, tomato sauce, garlic, mustard, molasses, lemon juice, chili powder, paprika, and cayenne pepper in the bottom of the pot.
2. Place the chicken and move the chicken around in the sauce with tongs to coat evenly.
3. Close the lid and move slider to AIR FRY/STOVETOP. Select SLOW COOK, set temperature to Lo, and set time to 7 hours. Press START/STOP to begin cooking, until the chicken registers 165°F on a food thermometer
4. When cooking is complete, let cool for 5 minutes and serve warm.

Spiced Turkey Tenderloin

SERVES: 4

PREP TIME: 20 minutes
COOK TIME: 30 minutes

Olive oil spray
1½ pounds (680 g) turkey breast tenderloin
½ tsp. garlic powder
½ tsp. paprika
½ tsp. salt
½ tsp. freshly ground black pepper
Pinch cayenne pepper

1. Close the lid and move slider to the AIR FRY/STOVETOP. Preheat the pot by selecting BAKE/ROAST, setting temperature to 375°F, and setting time to 5 minutes. Select START/STOP to begin preheating.
2. While unit is preheating, combine the paprika, garlic powder, salt, black pepper, and cayenne pepper in a small bowl. Rub the mixture all over the turkey.
3. Place the Foodi Smart Thermometer in the center of the thickest part of the meat.
4. When the pot has preheated, spray the bottom rack with olive oil spray and arrange the turkey. Place the rack with turkey in the pot. Close the lid and make sure the slider is still in the AIR FRY/STOVETOP.
5. Select BAKE/ROAST, set temperature to 375°F, then select PRESET. Use the arrows to the right of the display to select CHICKEN. Press START/STOP to begin cooking.
6. When cooking is complete, remove the rack with turkey and let cool for 10 minutes before slicing and serving.

Cheese Chicken Breasts and Tomatoes

SERVES: 4

PREP: 5 minutes
TOTAL COOK TIME: 30 minutes
PRESSURE BUILD: approx. 15 minutes
COOK: 15 minutes

4 large boneless chicken breasts
1 cup water
16 ounces (454 g) fresh mozzarella cheese, sliced
8 tomato slices
½ tbsp.garlic powder
Salt and freshly ground black pepper
Fresh basil, for serving

1. Place the chicken breasts, 1 cup water, garlic powder, salt, and black pepper in the pot.
2. Close lid and move slider to PRESSURE. Make sure the pressure release valve is in the SEAL position.
3. The temperature will default to HIGH, which is the correct setting. Select QUICK RELEASE. Set time to 10 minutes. Select START/STOP to begin cooking (the unit will build pressure for approx. 15 minutes before cooking begins).
4. When cooking is complete and the pressure automatically releases, select START/STOP and move slider to AIR FRY/STOVETOP to unlock the lid, then carefully open it.
5. Carefully remove the chicken breasts and drain any remaining water. Wipe out the pot. Place the bottom rack in the pot. Arrange the chicken breasts on the rack. Top each with the tomato and mozzarella cheese slices.
6. Close lid and keep slider in the AIR FRY/STOVETOP position. Select BROIL, set temperature to 450°F and set time to 5 minutes. Select START/STOP to begin cooking.
7. Once the cheese has melted, serve immediately with a sprinkle of fresh basil.

Kadai Chicken with Carrot

SERVES: 4

PREP TIME: 10 minutes COOK TIME: 5 minutes	2 tbsps. ghee 1 pound (454 g) boneless chicken thighs, cut into 1-inch pieces 1 medium carrot, roll-cut into ½-inch pieces 1 medium onion, cut into 1-inch pieces 2 chiles, sliced into ¼-inch circles (no need to core or seed them) 2 garlic cloves, crushed and chopped ½ cup whole-milk Greek yogurt 1 tbsp. ginger, crushed and chopped 1 tsp. ground coriander 1 tsp. cumin 1 tsp. paprika

1. Close lid and move slider to AIR FRY/STOVETOP. Select SEAR/SAUTÉ and set to Hi5. Open lid and select START/STOP to begin preheating. Allow unit to preheat for 5 minutes.
2. After 5 minutes, heat the ghee in the pot until it shimmers.
3. Add the garlic, ginger, chicken and carrot and sear for about 1 minute.
4. Put the onion, coriander, cumin, and paprika and sauté for about 1 minute.
5. Then place the sliced chiles and sauté for about 1 minute.
6. Press START/STOP to turn off the cooker and stir the yogurt into the pot. Serve hot.

Yummy Stuffed Chicken Breast with Fettuccine

SERVES: 4

PREP: 15 minutes TOTAL COOK TIME: 27 minutes STEAM: approx. 12 minutes COOK: 15 minutes	LEVEL 1 (BOTTOM OF POT) 8 ounces fettuccine, broken in half 2 cups fresh spinach leaves 2 cups water or stock 1 (15 ounces) canned alfredo sauce LEVEL 2 (TOP RACK) 2 (8-ounce) chicken fillets, skinless and boneless, each cut into 2 pieces 4 brie cheese slices 4 cured ham slices 1 tbsp. chive, minced Salt and black pepper, to taste TOPPINGS: Hummus Tzatziki Fresh herbs

1. Place all Level 1 ingredients in the pot and stir until combined.
2. Make a slit in each chicken piece horizontally and season with the salt and black pepper.
3. Insert cheese slice in the slits and sprinkle with chives. Wrap each chicken piece with one ham slice.
4. Place the top rack in the pot, then place the wrapped chicken on the rack. Close the lid and move slider to STEAM-CRISP position.
5. Select STEAM & CRISP, set temperature to 390°F, and set time to 15 minutes. Press START/STOP to begin cooking (PrE will display for approx. 12 minutes as the unit steams, then the timer will start counting down).
6. When cooking is complete, remove the rack with the wrapped chicken. Stir the spinach and serve with chicken and desired toppings.

CHAPTER 9
SNACK

Rosemary Fingerling Potatoes / 59

Air Fried Pot Stickers / 59

Classic Onion Rings / 60

Healthy Kiwi Slices / 60

Spicy Chicken Bites / 61

Dried Dragon Fruit Chips / 61

Chicken and Pepper Meatballs / 62

Classic Mozzarella Arancini / 62

Crispy Green Olives / 63

Tasty Strawberry Slices / 63

Cheesy Dinner Rolls / 63

Breaded Artichoke Hearts / 64

Homemade Salmon Croquettes / 64

Spicy Kale Chips / 64

Rosemary Fingerling Potatoes

SERVES: 3

PREP TIME: 10 minutes
COOK TIME: 48 minutes

8 ounces fingerling potatoes
1 sprig rosemary
1 tbsp. unsalted vegan butter
Salt, and pepper to taste

1. Add 12 cups of room-temperature water to the pot.
2. Close the lid and move slider to AIR FRY/STOVETOP, then use the dial to select SOUS VIDE. Select SOUS VIDE, set temperature to 190°F, and set time to 45 minutes.
3. Press START/STOP to begin preheating.
4. Season the potatoes with salt and pepper and transfer them to a re-sealable zip bag.
5. When preheating is complete and "ADD FOOD" will show on the display.
6. Open the lid and place bag in the water using the water displacement method. When just the bag's seal is above the water line, finish closing the bag, making sure no water gets inside. Keep the bag's seal just above the water line. Close the lid.
7. When cooking is complete, remove the bag with potatoes from cooker. Cut the potatoes in half (lengthwise).
8. In a large skillet over medium-high heat, melt the butter and add the rosemary and potatoes. Cook for about 3 minutes and transfer to a plate.
9. Serve by seasoning it with a bit of salt if needed.

Air Fried Pot Stickers

MAKES: 24 POT STICKERS

PREP TIME: 10 minutes
COOK TIME: 20 minutes

cooking spray
24 wonton wrappers
1 egg, beaten
½ cup finely chopped cabbage
¼ cup finely chopped red bell pepper
2 green onions, finely chopped
2 tbsps. cocktail sauce
1 tbsp. water, for brushing the wrappers
2 tsps. low-sodium soy sauce

1. Close the lid and move slider to the AIR FRY/STOVETOP. Preheat the pot by selecting AIR FRY, setting temperature to 390°F, and setting time to 5 minutes. Select START/STOP to begin preheating.
2. While unit is preheating, in a small bowl, combine the cabbage, pepper, green onions, egg, cocktail sauce, and soy sauce, and mix well.
3. Put about 1 tsp. mixture in the center of each wonton wrapper. Fold the wrapper in half, covering the filling; dampen the edges with water, and seal. You can crimp the edges of the wrapper with your fingers so they look like the pot stickers you get in restaurants. Brush them with water.
4. Attach Cook & Crisp Basket with diffuser and spray with cooking spray, then add half of the pot stickers.
5. When the pot has preheated, place the basket in the pot. Close the lid and make sure the slider is still in the AIR FRY/STOVETOP.
6. Select AIR FRY, set temperature to 390°F, and set time to 10 minutes. Select START/STOP to begin cooking, until the pot stickers are hot and the bottoms are lightly browned.
7. Repeat with the remaining pot stickers.
8. When cooking is complete, remove the basket and serve hot.

Classic Onion Rings

SERVES: 4

PREP TIME: 10 minutes
COOK TIME: 10 minutes

cooking spray
1 large onion, cut into rings
1 egg
1¼ cups all-purpose flour
1 cup milk
¾ cup dry bread crumbs
Salt, to taste

1. Mix together flour and salt in a dish. Whisk the egg with milk in a second dish until well mixed. Add the breadcrumbs in a third dish.
2. Coat the onion rings evenly with the flour mixture and dip into the egg mixture. Then dredge in the breadcrumbs.
3. Close the lid and move slider to the AIR FRY/STOVETOP. Preheat the pot by selecting AIR FRY, setting temperature to 390°F, and setting time to 5 minutes. Select START/STOP to begin preheating, attach Cook & Crisp Basket with diffuser and spray with cooking spray, then arrange the onion rings in a single layer.
4. When the pot has preheated, place the basket in the pot. Close the lid and make sure the slider is still in the AIR FRY/STOVETOP.
5. Select AIR FRY, set temperature to 390°F, and set time to 10 minutes. Select START/STOP to begin cooking, flipping halfway through cooking.
6. When cooking is complete, remove the basket and serve hot.

Healthy Kiwi Slices

SERVES: 4

PREP TIME: 20 minutes
COOK TIME: 8 hours

spray bottle of lemon juice
4 medium kiwi fruits, peeled and sliced as thinly as you can

1. Spray the kiwi slices lightly with lemon juice.
2. Place the bottom rack in the pot. Lay half of the kiwi slices on the rack. Place the top rack in the pot. Lay the remaining kiwi slices on the top rack. Make sure none of the slices are touching one another.
3. Close the lid and move the slider slider to AIR FRY/STOVETOP. Select DEHYDRATE, set temperature to 135°F, and set time to 8 hours. Press START/STOP to begin cooking.
4. When cooking is complete, remove the racks with the kiwi slices. Store in an airtight container.

Spicy Chicken Bites

PREP: 10 minutes
TOTAL COOK TIME: 21 minutes
STEAM: approx. 6 minutes
COOK: 15 minutes

½ cup water, for steaming
cooking spray
8 ounces boneless and skinless chicken thighs, cut into 30 pieces
2 tbsps. hot sauce
¼ tsp. kosher salt

1. Season the chicken bites with kosher salt.
2. Add ½ cup water to the pot. Spray the Cook & Crisp Basket with cooking spray, then place the basket in the pot. Add the chicken bites to the basket, spreading it evenly across the basket. Close the lid and move slider to STEAMCRISP.
3. Select STEAM & CRISP, set temperature to 390°F, and set time to 15 minutes. Press START/STOP to begin cooking (PrE will display for approx. 6 minutes as the unit steams, then the timer will start counting down).
4. With 8 minutes remaining, open the lid and toss the chicken bites with tongs. Close the lid to continue cooking.
5. When the cooking is complete, remove the basket from pot. Transfer the bites to the sauce bowl, tossing to coat evenly. Serve hot.

Dried Dragon Fruit Chips

PREP TIME: 20 minutes
COOK TIME: 6 hours

3 large Dragon Fruits, washed thoroughly, cut into ¼-inch slices and left the skin on the fruit (can hold the slices together)

1. Place the bottom rack in the pot. Lay half of fruit slices flat on the rack. Place the top rack in the pot. Lay the remaining fruit slices flat on the top rack. Make sure none of the slices are touching one another.
2. Close the lid and move the slider slider to AIR FRY/STOVETOP. Select DEHYDRATE, set temperature to 135°F, and set time to 6 hours. Press START/STOP to begin cooking.
3. When cooking is complete, remove the racks with the fruit slices. Store in an airtight container.

Chicken and Pepper Meatballs

MAKES: 16 MEATBALLS

PREP: 5 minutes
TOTAL COOK TIME: 22-24 minutes
STEAM: approx. 6 minutes
COOK: 16-18 minutes

1 cup water, for steaming
2 tsps. olive oil
½ pound (227 g) ground chicken breast
1 egg white
¼ cup minced red bell pepper
¼ cup minced onion
2 vanilla wafers, crushed
½ tsp. dried thyme

1. In a skillet, add the olive oil, onion, and red bell pepper over medium heat. Sauté for about 3 to 5 minutes, until the vegetables are tender.
2. In a medium bowl, mix the cooked vegetables, egg white, crushed wafers, and thyme until well combined.
3. Mix the chicken, gently but thoroughly, until everything is combined. Form the chicken mixture into 16 meatballs.
4. Add ½ cup water to the pot. Spray the Cook & Crisp Basket with cooking spray, then place the basket in the pot. Add the meatballs to the basket, spreading it evenly across the basket. Close the lid and move slider to STEAM-CRISP.
5. Select STEAM & CRISP, set temperature to 350°F, and set time to 13 minutes. Press START/STOP to begin cooking (PrE will display for approx. 6 minutes as the unit steams, then the timer will start counting down).
6. With 6 minutes remaining, open the lid and flip the meatballs with tongs. Close the lid to continue cooking.
7. When the cooking is complete, remove the basket from pot. Serve immediately.

Classic Mozzarella Arancini

MAKES: 16 ARANCINI

PREP TIME: 5 minutes
COOK TIME: 10 minutes

2 tbsps. olive oil
2 cups cooked rice, cooled
2 eggs, beaten
16 (¾-inch) cubes Mozzarella cheese
1½ cups panko bread crumbs, divided
½ cup grated Parmesan cheese
2 tbsps. minced fresh basil

1. Close the lid and move slider to the AIR FRY/STOVETOP. Preheat the pot by selecting AIR FRY, setting temperature to 400°F, and setting time to 5 minutes. Select START/STOP to begin preheating.
2. While unit is preheating, in a medium bowl, combine the rice, eggs, ½ cup bread crumbs, Parmesan cheese, and basil. Form this rice mixture into 16 (1½-inch) balls.
3. Poke a hole in each of the balls with your finger and insert a Mozzarella cube. Form the rice mixture firmly around the cheese.
4. On a shallow plate, mix the remaining 1 cup bread crumbs with the olive oil and combine well. Roll the rice balls in the bread crumbs to coat.
5. Attach Cook & Crisp Basket with diffuser and spray with cooking spray, then add the arancini.
6. When the pot has preheated, place the basket in the pot. Close the lid and make sure the slider is still in the AIR FRY/STOVETOP.
7. Select AIR FRY, set temperature to 400°F, and set time to 10 minutes. Select START/STOP to begin cooking, until golden brown.
8. When cooking is complete, remove the basket and transfer the arancini to a plate. Serve hot.

Crispy Green Olives

PREP TIME: 5 minutes COOK TIME: 8 minutes	Cooking spray 1 (5½-ounce / 156-g) jar pitted green olives 1 egg ½ cup all-purpose flour ½ cup bread crumbs Salt and pepper, to taste

1. Remove the green olives from the jar and dry thoroughly with paper towels.
2. In a small bowl, combine the flour with salt and black pepper to taste. Place the bread crumbs in another small bowl. In a third small bowl, beat the egg.
3. Dip the green olives in the flour, then the egg, and then the bread crumbs.
4. Close the lid and move slider to the AIR FRY/STOVETOP. Preheat the pot by selecting AIR FRY, setting temperature to 400°F, and setting time to 5 minutes. Select START/STOP to begin preheating.
5. While unit is preheating, attach Cook & Crisp Basket with diffuser and spray with cooking spray, then add the breaded olives.
6. When the pot has preheated, place the basket in the pot. Close the lid and make sure the slider is still in the AIR FRY/STOVETOP.
7. Select AIR FRY, set temperature to 400°F, and set time to 8 minutes. Select START/STOP to begin cooking, tossing halfway through cooking.
8. When cooking is complete, remove the basket and let cool before serving.

Tasty Strawberry Slices

PREP TIME: 20 minutes COOK TIME: 7 hours	spray bottle of lemon juice 1 pound strawberries, washed and hulled, then thin sliced

1. Lightly spray the strawberries with lemon juice.
2. Place the bottom rack in the pot. Lay half of the strawberries on the rack. Place the top rack in the pot. Lay the remaining strawberries on the top rack. Make sure none of the slices are touching one another.
3. Close the lid and move the slider slider to AIR FRY/STOVETOP. Select DEHYDRATE, set temperature to 135°F, and set time to 7 hours. Press START/STOP to begin cooking.
4. When cooking is complete, remove the racks with the strawberries. Store in an airtight container.

Cheesy Dinner Rolls

PREP: 10 minutes TOTAL COOK TIME: 14 minutes STEAM: approx. 6 minutes COOK: 8 minutes	1 cup water, for steaming cooking spray 2 tbsps. unsalted butter, melted 2 dinner rolls ½ cup Parmesan cheese, grated ½ tsp. garlic bread seasoning mix

1. Pour 1 cup water into the pot. Spray the bottom of the Ninja Multi-Purpose Pan with cooking spray, avoiding the sides.
2. Cut the dinner rolls in slits and stuff cheese in the slits. Top with butter and garlic bread seasoning mix.
3. Arrange the dinner rolls to the prepared pan.
4. Place the pan on the bottom rack, then place the rack in the pot. Close the lid and move slider to STEAMCRISP.
5. Select STEAM & BAKE, set temperature to 350°F, and set time to 8 minutes. Press START/STOP to begin cooking (PrE will display for approx. 6 minutes as the unit steams, then the timer will start counting down).
6. When cooking is complete, remove the rack with the pan and serve hot.

Breaded Artichoke Hearts

PREP TIME: 5 minutes COOK TIME: 8 minutes	Cooking spray 1 egg 14 whole artichoke hearts, packed in water	½ cup all-purpose flour ⅓ cup panko bread crumbs 1 tsp. Italian seasoning

1. Squeeze excess water from the artichoke hearts and arrange on paper towels to dry.
2. In a small bowl, beat the egg. In another small bowl, add the flour. In a third small bowl, mix the panko bread crumbs and Italian seasoning, and stir well.
3. Dip the artichoke hearts in the flour, then the egg, and then the bread crumb mixture.
4. Close the lid and move slider to the AIR FRY/STOVETOP. Preheat the pot by selecting AIR FRY, setting temperature to 390°F, and setting time to 5 minutes. Select START/STOP to begin preheating.
5. While unit is preheating, attach Cook & Crisp Basket with diffuser and spray with cooking spray, then add the breaded artichoke hearts.
6. When the pot has preheated, place the basket in the pot. Close the lid and make sure the slider is still in the AIR FRY/STOVETOP.
7. Select AIR FRY, set temperature to 390°F, and set time to 8 minutes. Select START/STOP to begin cooking, flipping halfway through cooking.
8. When cooking is complete, remove the basket and let cool for 5 minutes, then serve warm.

Homemade Salmon Croquettes

PREP: 15 minutes TOTAL COOK TIME: 16 minutes STEAM: approx. 8 minutes COOK: 8 minutes	½ cup water, for steaming ⅓ cup vegetable oil 1 large can red salmon, drained 2 eggs, lightly beaten	1 cup breadcrumbs 2 tbsps. fresh parsley, chopped 2 tbsps. milk Salt and black pepper, to taste

1. Mash the salmon completely in a large bowl and stir in the eggs, milk, parsley, salt and black pepper.
2. Mix until well combined and make 16 equal-sized croquettes from the salmon mixture.
3. Combine together vegetable oil and breadcrumbs in a shallow dish and coat the croquettes in this mixture.
4. Add ½ cup water to the pot. Spray the Cook & Crisp Basket with cooking spray, then place the basket in the pot. Add the croquettes to the basket, spreading it evenly across the basket. Close the lid and move slider to STEAMCRISP.
5. Select STEAM & CRISP, set temperature to 400°F, and set time to 8 minutes. Press START/STOP to begin cooking (PrE will display for approx. 8 minutes as the unit steams, then the timer will start counting down).
6. With 4 minutes remaining, open the lid and flip the croquettes with tongs. Close the lid to continue cooking.
7. When the cooking is complete, remove the basket from pot. Transfer the croquettes into a serving bowl and serve warm.

Spicy Kale Chips

PREP TIME: 5 minutes COOK TIME: 8 minutes	Cooking spray 2 tsps. canola oil 5 cups kale, large stems removed and chopped	¼ tsp. smoked paprika ¼ tsp. kosher salt

1. Close the lid and move slider to the AIR FRY/STOVETOP. Preheat the pot by selecting AIR FRY, setting temperature to 300°F, and setting time to 5 minutes. Select START/STOP to begin preheating.
2. While unit is preheating, in a large bowl, toss the canola oil, kale, smoked paprika, and kosher salt.
3. Attach Cook & Crisp Basket with diffuser and spray with cooking spray, then add the kale.
4. When the pot has preheated, place the basket in the pot. Close the lid and make sure the slider is still in the AIR FRY/STOVETOP.
5. Select AIR FRY, set temperature to 300°F, and set time to 8 minutes. Select START/STOP to begin cooking, tossing halfway through cooking.
6. When cooking is complete, remove the basket and let cool on a wire rack for 3 to 5 minutes before serving.

CHAPTER 10
DESSERT

Apple and Pear Crisp / 66

Tasty Double Chocolate Muffins / 66

Red Velvet Cupcakes / 67

Simple Blueberry Cake / 67

Creamy Chocolate Cake / 68

Homemade Shortbread Fingers / 68

Apple Dumplings with Raisin / 69

Walnut Chocolate Brownies / 69

Candied Eggnog Bread / 70

Simple Pineapple Sticks / 70

Healthy Fruit Muffins / 71

Peach Brown Betty with Cranberries / 71

Pumpkin Pudding / 72

Black Forest Pies / 72

Apple and Pear Crisp

SERVES: 6

PREP TIME: 10 minutes
COOK TIME: 20 minutes

cooking spray
½ pound (227 g) apples, cored and chopped
½ pound (227 g) pears, cored and chopped
1 cup sugar
1 cup flour
¼ cup chopped walnuts

1 tbsp. butter
1 tsp. ground cinnamon
1 tsp. vanilla extract
¼ tsp. ground cloves
Whipped cream, for serving

1. Close the lid and move slider to the AIR FRY/STOVETOP. Preheat the pot by selecting BAKE/ROAST, setting temperature to 350°F, and setting time to 5 minutes. Select START/STOP to begin preheating.
2. While unit is preheating, spray the Ninja Multi-Purpose Pan with cooking spray, then add the apples and pears.
3. Combine the remaining ingredients, minus the walnuts and the whipped cream, until a coarse, crumbly texture is achieved.
4. Pour the mixture over the fruits and spread evenly. Top with the chopped walnuts.
5. Place the pan on the bottom rack. When the pot has preheated, place the rack with pan in the pot. Close the lid and make sure the slider is still in the AIR FRY/STOVETOP.
6. Select BAKE/ROAST, set temperature to 350°F, and set time to 20 minutes. Select START/STOP to begin cooking, until the top turns golden brown.
7. When cooking is complete, remove the rack with the pan and let cool for 20 minutes. Serve at room temperature with whipped cream.

Tasty Double Chocolate Muffins

SERVES: 12

PREP: 20 minutes
TOTAL COOK TIME: 45 minutes
STEAM: approx. 20 minutes
COOK: 25 minutes

1 cup water, for steaming
cooking spray
1⅓ cups self-rising flour
⅔ cup plus 3 tbsps. caster sugar
3½ ounces butter

2½ ounces milk chocolate, finely chopped
5 tbsps. milk
2½ tbsps. cocoa powder
½ tsp. vanilla extract

1. Pour 1 cup water into the pot. Spray 12 muffin molds with cooking spray.
2. Mix the flour, sugar, and cocoa powder in a medium bowl.
3. Stir in the butter, milk, vanilla extract and chopped chocolate and combine until well mixed.
4. Transfer the mixture evenly into the muffin molds.
5. Place the bottom rack in the pot and arrange 6 muffin molds. Put the top rack on the pot and add the remaining 6 muffin molds. Close the lid and move slider to STEAMCRISP.
6. Select STEAM & BAKE, set temperature to 315°F, and set time to 25 minutes. Press START/STOP to begin cooking (PrE will display for approx. 20 minutes as the unit steams, then the timer will start counting down).
7. When cooking is complete, remove the rack with the muffin molds. Let cool for 5 minutes before serving.

Red Velvet Cupcakes

SERVES: 12

PREP: 15 minutes
TOTAL COOK TIME: 36 minutes
STEAM: approx. 20 minutes
COOK: 16 minutes

1 cup water, for steaming
cooking spray
FOR THE CUPCAKES:
3 eggs
2 cups refined flour
¾ cup peanut butter
¾ cup icing sugar
2 tsps. beet powder

1 tsp. cocoa powder
FOR THE FROSTING:
1 cup cream cheese
1 cup butter
¾ cup icing sugar
¼ cup strawberry sauce
1 tsp. vanilla essence

1. Pour 1 cup water into the pot. Spray 12 silicon cups with cooking spray.
2. In a large bowl, mix all the cupcakes ingredients until well combined.
3. Transfer the mixture into the silicon cups.
4. Place the bottom rack in the pot and arrange 6 silicon cups. Put the top rack on the pot and add the remaining 6 silicon cups. Close the lid and move slider to STEAMCRISP.
5. Select STEAM & BAKE, set temperature to 350°F, and set time to 16 minutes. Press START/STOP to begin cooking (PrE will display for approx. 20 minutes as the unit steams, then the timer will start counting down).
6. Meanwhile, mix all the frosting ingredients in a large bowl until well combined.
7. When cooking is complete, remove the rack with the silicon cups. Top each cupcake evenly with frosting and serve.

Simple Blueberry Cake

SERVES: 6

PREP: 10 minutes
TOTAL COOK TIME: 40 minutes
STEAM: approx. 20 minutes
COOK: 20 minutes

2 cups water, for steaming
cooking spray
1 stick butter, room temperature
3 eggs
1 cup almond flour
⅔ cup swerve
½ cup sour cream
⅓ cup blueberries
1½ tsps. baking powder
2 tsps. vanilla

1. Pour 2 cups water into the pot. Spray the bottom of the Ninja Multi-Purpose Pan with cooking spray, avoiding the sides.
2. Mix all the ingredients in a bowl except the blueberries.
3. Pour the batter in the prepared pan and gently fold in the blueberries.
4. Place the pan on the bottom rack, then place the rack in the pot. Close the lid and move slider to STEAMCRISP.
5. Select STEAM & BAKE, set temperature to 350°F, and set time to 20 minutes. Press START/STOP to begin cooking (PrE will display for approx. 20 minutes as the unit steams, then the timer will start counting down).
6. When cooking is complete, remove the rack with the pan and let cool for about 5 minutes. Cut into slices to serve.

Creamy Chocolate Cake

SERVES: 4

PREP: 10 minutes
TOTAL COOK TIME: 50 minutes
STEAM: approx. 20 minutes
COOK: 30 minutes

3 cups water, for steaming
Unsalted butter, at room temperature
3 large eggs
⅔ cup sugar
1 cup almond flour
⅓ cup heavy cream
¼ cup coconut oil, melted
¼ cup unsweetened cocoa powder
¼ cup chopped walnuts
1 tsp. baking powder

1. Pour 3 cups water into the pot. Generously butter a 8-inch round baking pan. Line the bottom of the pan with parchment paper cut to fit.
2. In a large bowl, mix the almond flour, eggs, cream, sugar, coconut oil, cocoa powder, and baking powder.
3. Beat with a hand mixer on medium speed until well blended and fluffy. Gently fold in the walnuts. Pour the batter into the prepared pan.
4. Place the pan on the bottom rack, then place the rack in the pot. Close the lid and move slider to STEAMCRISP.
5. Select STEAM & BAKE, set temperature to 390°F, and set time to 30 minutes. Press START/STOP to begin cooking (PrE will display for approx. 20 minutes as the unit steams, then the timer will start counting down), until a knife (do not use a toothpick) inserted into the center of the cake comes out clean.
6. When cooking is complete, remove the rack with the pan and let cool for 30 minutes before slicing and serving.

Homemade Shortbread Fingers

SERVES: 10

PREP TIME: 10 minutes
COOK TIME: 12 minutes

cooking spray
¾ cup butter
1⅓ cups plain flour
⅓ cup caster sugar

1. Close the lid and move slider to the AIR FRY/STOVETOP. Preheat the pot by selecting BAKE/ROAST, setting temperature to 350°F, and setting time to 5 minutes. Select START/STOP to begin preheating.
2. While unit is preheating, spray the Ninja Multi-Purpose Pan with cooking spray.
3. In a bowl, mix the sugar, flour and butter to form a dough.
4. Cut the dough into 10 equal sized fingers and prick the fingers lightly with a fork.
5. Arrange the fingers on the prepared pan.
6. Place the pan on the bottom rack. When the pot has preheated, place the rack with pan in the pot. Close the lid and make sure the slider is still in the AIR FRY/STOVETOP.
7. Select BAKE/ROAST, set temperature to 350°F, and set time to 12 minutes. Select START/STOP to begin cooking.
8. When cooking is complete, remove the rack with the pan and let cool for 10 minutes. Serve warm.

Apple Dumplings with Raisin

SERVES: 2

PREP TIME: 10 minutes
COOK TIME: 15 minutes

cooking spray
2 small apples, peeled and cored
2 sheets puff pastry
2 tbsps. butter, melted
2 tbsps. raisins
1 tbsp. brown sugar

1. Close the lid and move slider to the AIR FRY/STOVETOP. Preheat the pot by selecting AIR FRY, setting temperature to 390°F, and setting time to 5 minutes. Select START/STOP to begin preheating.
2. While unit is preheating, mix the sugar and raisins in a small bowl and fill each apple core with it.
3. Put the apple in the center of each pastry sheet and fold to completely cover the apple. Seal the edges.
4. Attach Cook & Crisp Basket with diffuser and spray with cooking spray, then arrange the dumplings.
5. When the pot has preheated, place the basket in the pot. Close the lid and make sure the slider is still in the AIR FRY/STOVETOP.
6. Select AIR FRY, set temperature to 390°F, and set time to 15 minutes. Select START/STOP to begin cooking, flipping halfway through cooking.
7. When cooking is complete, remove the basket and serve hot.

Walnut Chocolate Brownies

SERVES: 8

PREP: 10 minutes
TOTAL COOK TIME: 35 minutes
STEAM: approx. 20 minutes
COOK: 15 minutes

1 cup water, for steaming
1 large egg, beaten
½ cup chocolate, chopped roughly
⅓ cup butter
¼ cup walnuts, chopped
5 tbsps. self-rising flour
5 tbsps. sugar
1 tsp. vanilla extract
Pinch of salt

1. Pour 1 cup water into the pot. Line a 8-inch round baking pan with greased parchment paper.
2. Microwave the chocolate and butter on high for 2 minutes.
3. Mix the egg, vanilla extract, sugar, salt and chocolate mixture in a bowl until well combined.
4. Stir in the flour mixture gently and fold in the walnuts.
5. Pour this mixture into the prepared pan and smooth the top surface of mixture with the back of spatula.
6. Place the pan on the bottom rack, then place the rack in the pot. Close the lid and move slider to STEAMCRISP.
7. Select STEAM & BAKE, set temperature to 350°F, and set time to 15 minutes. Press START/STOP to begin cooking (PrE will display for approx. 20 minutes as the unit steams, then the timer will start counting down).
8. When cooking is complete, remove the rack with the pan and let cool for at least 5 minutes. Cut into 8 equal sized squares to serve.

Candied Eggnog Bread

PREP: 10 minutes
TOTAL COOK TIME: 38 minutes
STEAM: approx. 20 minutes
COOK: 18 minutes

2 cups water, for steaming
Cooking spray
1 cup flour, plus more for dusting
½ cup eggnog
1 egg yolk
¼ cup pecans
¼ cup chopped candied fruit (cherries, pineapple, or mixed fruits)
¼ cup sugar
1 tbsp. plus 1 tsp. butter, melted
1 tsp. baking powder
¼ tsp. salt
¼ tsp. nutmeg

1. Pour 2 cups water into the pot. Spray the bottom of the Ninja Multi-Purpose Pan with cooking spray, avoiding the sides. Dust with flour.
2. In a medium bowl, stir together the flour, baking powder, sugar, salt, and nutmeg.
3. Add the eggnog, egg yolk, and butter. Mix well but do not beat. Stir in pecans and candied fruit.
4. Spread the batter evenly into prepared pan.
5. Place the pan on the bottom rack, then place the rack in the pot. Close the lid and move slider to STEAMCRISP.
6. Select STEAM & BAKE, set temperature to 350°F, and set time to 18 minutes. Press START/STOP to begin cooking (PrE will display for approx. 20 minutes as the unit steams, then the timer will start counting down).
7. When cooking is complete, remove the rack with the pan and let cool for at least 10 minutes. Serve immediately.

Simple Pineapple Sticks

PREP TIME: 5 minutes
COOK TIME: 10 minutes

cooking spray
½ fresh pineapple, cut into sticks
¼ cup desiccated coconut

1. Coat the pineapple sticks evenly with the desiccated coconut.
2. Close the lid and move slider to the AIR FRY/STOVETOP. Preheat the pot by selecting AIR FRY, setting temperature to 350°F, and setting time to 5 minutes. Select START/STOP to begin preheating.
3. While unit is preheating, attach Cook & Crisp Basket with diffuser and spray with cooking spray, then add the pineapple sticks in a single layer.
4. When the pot has preheated, place the basket in the pot. Close the lid and make sure the slider is still in the AIR FRY/STOVETOP.
5. Select AIR FRY, set temperature to 350°F, and set time to 10 minutes. Select START/STOP to begin cooking, flipping halfway through cooking.
6. When cooking is complete, remove the basket and serve hot.

Healthy Fruit Muffins

SERVES: 6

PREP TIME: 10 minutes COOK TIME: 10 minutes	1 pack Oreo biscuits, crushed 1 banana, peeled and chopped 1 apple, peeled, cored and chopped 1 cup milk 1 tsp. honey 1 tsp. cocoa powder 1 tsp. fresh lemon juice ¾ tsp. baking soda ¾ tsp. baking powder Pinch of ground cinnamon

1. Close the lid and move slider to the AIR FRY/STOVETOP. Preheat the pot by selecting BAKE/ROAST, setting temperature to 350°F, and setting time to 5 minutes. Select START/STOP to begin preheating.
2. While unit is preheating, spray 6 muffin cups with cooking spray.
3. Mix the milk, biscuits, cocoa powder, baking soda and baking powder in a bowl until a smooth mixture is formed.
4. Divide this mixture evenly into the prepared muffin cups.
5. Place the muffin cups on the bottom rack. When the pot has preheated, place the rack with muffin cups in the pot. Close the lid and make sure the slider is still in the AIR FRY/STOVETOP.
6. Select BAKE/ROAST, set temperature to 350°F, and set time to 10 minutes. Select START/STOP to begin cooking.
7. When cooking is complete, remove the rack with the muffin cups and let cool for 5 minutes.
8. Meanwhile, mix the banana, apple, honey, lemon juice and cinnamon in a bowl. Ladle some portion from center of muffins and fill with the fruit mixture.
9. Refrigerate for about 2 hours and serve chilled.

Peach Brown Betty with Cranberries

SERVES: 10

PREP TIME: 20 minutes COOK TIME: 6 hours	8 ripe peaches, peeled and cut into chunks 1 cup dried cranberries 3 cups cubed whole-wheat bread 1½ cups whole-wheat bread crumbs ⅓ cup coconut sugar ⅓ cup melted coconut oil 3 tbsps. honey 2 tbsps. freshly squeezed lemon juice ¼ tsp. ground cardamom

1. Mix the peaches, dried cranberries, lemon juice, and honey in the pot.
2. In a large bowl, mix the bread cubes, bread crumbs, coconut sugar, and cardamom. Pour the coconut oil over all and toss to coat evenly.
3. Place the bread mixture on the fruit in the pot.
4. Close the lid and move slider to AIR FRY/STOVETOP. Select SLOW COOK, set temperature to Lo, and set time to 6 hours. Press START/STOP to begin cooking, until the fruit is bubbling and the topping is browned.
5. When cooking is complete, let cool for about 5 minutes and serve warm.

Pumpkin Pudding

SERVES: 4

PREP: 10 minutes
TOTAL COOK TIME: 30 minutes
STEAM: approx. 20 minutes
COOK: 10 minutes

1 cup water, for steaming
cooking spray
3 cups pumpkin purée
2 eggs
1 cup full-fat cream
1 cup sugar
3 tbsps. honey
1 tbsp. ginger
1 tbsp. cinnamon
1 tsp. clove
1 tsp. nutmeg

1. Pour 1 cup water into the pot. Spray the bottom of the Ninja Multi-Purpose Pan with cooking spray, avoiding the sides.
2. In a bowl, mix all the ingredients together to combine well. Scrape the mixture into the prepared pan.
3. Place the pan on the bottom rack, then place the rack in the pot. Close the lid and move slider to STEAMCRISP.
4. Select STEAM & BAKE, set temperature to 390°F, and set time to 10 minutes. Press START/STOP to begin cooking (PrE will display for approx. 20 minutes as the unit steams, then the timer will start counting down).
5. When cooking is complete, remove the rack with the pan and let cool for about 5 minutes. Serve warm.

Black Forest Pies

SERVES: 6

PREP: 10 minutes
TOTAL COOK TIME: 30 minutes
STEAM: approx. 15 minutes
COOK: 15 minutes

1 cup water, for steaming
cooking spray
1 (10-by-15-inch) sheet frozen puff pastry, thawed
1 egg white, beaten
2 tbsps. coconut sugar
3 tbsps. milk or dark chocolate chips
2 tbsps. thick, hot fudge sauce
2 tbsps. chopped dried cherries
½ tsp. cinnamon

1. Pour 1 cup water into the pot. Spray the bottom of the Ninja Multi-Purpose Pan with cooking spray, avoiding the sides.
2. In a small bowl, mix the chocolate chips, fudge sauce, and dried cherries.
3. Roll out the puff pastry on a floured surface. Cut into 6 squares by using a sharp knife.
4. Divide the chocolate chip mixture evenly into the center of each puff pastry square. Fold the squares in half to make triangles. Firmly press the edges with the tines of a fork to seal.
5. Brush the triangles on all sides sparingly with the beaten egg white. Sprinkle the tops with cinnamon and sugar. Transfer the triangles on the prepared pan.
6. Place the pan on the bottom rack, then place the rack in the pot. Close the lid and move slider to STEAMCRISP.
7. Select STEAM & BAKE, set temperature to 350°F, and set time to 15 minutes. Press START/STOP to begin cooking (PrE will display for approx. 15 minutes as the unit steams, then the timer will start counting down).
8. When cooking is complete, remove the rack with the pan and let cool for at least 20 minutes before serving.

APPENDIX 1:
4-WEEK MEAL PLAN

Week-1	Breakfast	Lunch	Dinner	Snack/Dessert
Day-1	Bacon and Spinach Cups	Beef Steak and Mushroom Alfredo Rice	Asparagus with Almond Slices	Homemade Shortbread Fingers
Day-2	Mediterranean Spinach Strata	Lemony Pork Chop and Leeks	Inspired Halibut	Rosemary Fingerling Potatoes
Day-3	Dill Zucchini Fritters	Authentic Mexican Street Corn	Thyme Lamb Chops	Red Velvet Cupcakes
Day-4	Veggie Frittata	Shishito Peppers with Dipping Sauce	Yummy Stuffed Chicken Breast with Fettuccine	Spicy Kale Chips
Day-5	Macaroni and Cheese	Garlic Squid	Sha Cha Beef with Sugar Snap	Walnut Chocolate Brownies
Day-6	Sweet Potato Hash	Breaded Pork Chops and Cherry Tomato Pasta	Shakshouka with Kale	Spicy Chicken Bites
Day-7	Cornflakes Toast Sticks	Spiced Lamb Satay	Confit Duck Leg with Cranberry Sauce	Crispy Green Olives

Week-2	Breakfast	Lunch	Dinner	Snack/Dessert
Day-1	Creamy Parsley Soufflé	Cheesy Barley Risotto with Mushroom	Classic Brisket Chili Verde	Tasty Strawberry Slices
Day-2	Ginger Chicken Porridge	Herbed Lamb Shoulder	Ginger Lentil Stew	Simple Blueberry Cake
Day-3	Nutty Baked Apples	Creamy Penne and Tuna Cakes	Italian Sausage Meatballs	Classic Onion Rings
Day-4	British Scotch Eggs	Vietnamese Caramelized Pork with Kimchi	Cheese Chicken Breasts and Tomatoes	Black Forest Pies
Day-5	Homemade Refried Black Beans	Tender Cabbage Wedges	Buttered Scallops	Tasty Double Chocolate Muffins
Day-6	Greek Pumpkin Bread	Corned Beef	Crunchy Fried Okra	Chicken and Pepper Meatballs
Day-7	Bacon Wrapped Sausage	Breaded Chicken Cutlets	Spiced Lamb Steaks and Snap Pea Rice	Apple and Pear Crisp

Week-3	Breakfast	Lunch	Dinner	Snack/Dessert
Day-1	British Scotch Eggs	Lamb Loin Chops with Mushroom Barley	Nutty Sprouts	Spicy Kale Chips
Day-2	Sweet Potato Hash	Chinese Eggplant and Pork	Parmesan Broccoli	Tasty Double Chocolate Muffins
Day-3	Cornflakes Toast Sticks	Garlic Lemon Butter Seared Scallops	Garlic Soy Chicken Thighs	Spicy Chicken Bites
Day-4	Ginger Chicken Porridge	Ginger Lentil Stew	Perfect Skirt Steak	Crispy Green Olives
Day-5	Dill Zucchini Fritters	Korean Style Pork Ribs	Salmon, Mushroom and Barley	Red Velvet Cupcakes
Day-6	Bacon and Spinach Cups	Crunchy Fried Okra	Buttered Ribeye Steak	Classic Onion Rings
Day-7	Nutty Baked Apples	Kadai Chicken with Carrot	Air Fried Lamb Ribs with Mint Yogurt	Homemade Shortbread Fingers

Week-4	Breakfast	Lunch	Dinner	Snack/Dessert
Day-1	Homemade Refried Black Beans	Beef and Veggie Kebabs	Little Bay Yellow Curry	Walnut Chocolate Brownies
Day-2	Bacon Wrapped Sausage	Spanish Garlic Shrimp	BBQ Flavored Pork Ribs	Tasty Strawberry Slices
Day-3	Creamy Parsley Soufflé	Cheesy Barley Risotto with Mushroom	Honey Beets and Red Onions	Black Forest Pies
Day-4	Macaroni and Cheese	Lime Lamb and Chiles	Vegan Nuggets	Rosemary Fingerling Potatoes
Day-5	Mediterranean Spinach Strata	Chili Chicken Dish	Thai Beef Roast and Veggies	Simple Blueberry Cake
Day-6	Veggie Frittata	Breaded Hake and Green Beans Meal	Pork Chops and Carrot	Chicken and Pepper Meatballs
Day-7	Greek Pumpkin Bread	Lamb Leg with Brussels Sprouts	Asparagus with Almond Slices	Apple and Pear Crisp

APPENDIX 2: BASIC KITCHEN CONVERSIONS & EQUIVALENTS

DRY MEASUREMENTS CONVERSION CHART

3 teaspoons = 1 tablespoon = 1/16 cup
6 teaspoons = 2 tablespoons = 1/8 cup
12 teaspoons = 4 tablespoons = ¼ cup
24 teaspoons = 8 tablespoons = ½ cup
36 teaspoons = 12 tablespoons = ¾ cup
48 teaspoons = 16 tablespoons = 1 cup

METRIC TO US COOKING CONVERSIONS

OVEN TEMPERATURES

120 °C = 250 °F
160 °C = 320 °F
180 °C = 350 °F
205 °C = 400 °F
220 °C = 425 °F

LIQUID MEASUREMENTS CONVERSION CHART

8 fluid ounces = 1 cup = ½ pint = ¼ quart
16 fluid ounces = 2 cups = 1 pint = ½ quart
32 fluid ounces = 4 cups = 2 pints = 1 quart = ¼ gallon
128 fluid ounces = 16 cups = 8 pints = 4 quarts = 1 gallon

BAKING IN GRAMS

1 cup flour = 140 grams
1 cup sugar = 150 grams
1 cup powdered sugar = 160 grams
1 cup heavy cream = 235 grams

VOLUME

1 milliliter = 1/5 teaspoon
5 ml = 1 teaspoon
15 ml = 1 tablespoon
240 ml = 1 cup or 8 fluid ounces
1 liter = 34 fluid ounces

WEIGHT

1 gram = .035 ounces
100 grams = 3.5 ounces
500 grams = 1.1 pounds
1 kilogram = 35 ounces

US TO METRIC COOKING CONVERSIONS

1/5 tsp = 1 ml
1 tsp = 5 ml
1 tbsp = 15 ml
1 fluid ounces = 30 ml
1 cup = 237 ml
1 pint (2 cups) = 473 ml
1 quart (4 cups) = .95 liter
1 gallon (16 cups) = 3.8 liters
1 oz = 28 grams
1 pound = 454 grams

BUTTER

1 cup butter = 2 sticks = 8 ounces = 230 grams = 16 tablespoons

WHAT DOES 1 CUP EQUAL

1 cup = 8 fluid ounces
1 cup = 16 tablespoons
1 cup = 48 teaspoons
1 cup = ½ pint
1 cup = ¼ quart
1 cup = 1/16 gallon
1 cup = 240 ml

BAKING PAN CONVERSIONS

9-inch round cake pan = 12 cups
10-inch tube pan =16 cups
10-inch bundt pan = 12 cups
9-inch springform pan = 10 cups
9 x 5 inch loaf pan = 8 cups
9-inch square pan = 8 cups

BAKING PAN CONVERSIONS

1 cup all-purpose flour = 4.5 oz
1 cup rolled oats = 3 oz
1 large egg = 1.7 oz
1 cup butter = 8 oz
1 cup milk = 8 oz
1 cup heavy cream = 8.4 oz
1 cup granulated sugar = 7.1 oz
1 cup packed brown sugar = 7.75 oz
1 cup vegetable oil = 7.7 oz
1 cup unsifted powdered sugar = 4.4 oz

APPENDIX 3:
RECIPES INDEX

A

Apple
Nutty Baked Apples / 14
Apple and Pear Crisp / 66
Apple Dumplings with Raisin / 69
Artichoke Heart
Breaded Artichoke Hearts / 64
Asparagus
Asparagus with Almond Slices / 24

B

Baby Back Rib
Korean Style Pork Ribs / 50
Air Fried Baby Back Ribs / 50
Baby Bella Mushroom
Veggie Frittata / 13
Banana
Healthy Fruit Muffins / 71
Beef
Beef Cheeseburgers / 38
Beef Brisket
Classic Brisket Chili Verde / 41
Barbecue Brisket Burnt Ends / 42
Beef Sirloin Roast
Classic Moroccan Beef Tagine / 41
Thai Beef Roast and Veggies / 43
Beef Steak
Beef Steak and Mushroom Alfredo Rice / 43
Beet
Honey Beets and Red Onions / 26
Black Bean
Homemade Refried Black Beans / 14
Blueberry
Simple Blueberry Cake / 67
Broccoli
Parmesan Broccoli / 23
Brussels Sprouts
Nutty Sprouts / 26
Button Mushroom
Cheesy Barley Risotto with Mushroom / 25

C

Cabbage
Tender Cabbage Wedges / 27
Air Fried Pot Stickers / 59
Chicken Breast
Chicken Nuggets / 52
Little Bay Yellow Curry / 55
Mediterranean Chicken with Sun-dried Tomato / 53

Cheese Chicken Breasts and Tomatoes / 56
Chili Chicken Dish / 55
Chicken and Pepper Meatballs / 62
Chicken Cutlet
Breaded Chicken Cutlets / 54
Chicken Fillet
Yummy Stuffed Chicken Breast with Fettuccine / 57
Chicken Thigh
Ginger Chicken Porridge / 9
Kadai Chicken with Carrot / 57
Jerk Chicken Thigh / 55
Garlic Soy Chicken Thighs / 54
Spicy Chicken Bites / 61
Chicken Wing
Simple Crispy Chicken Wings / 52
Chocolate Chip
Black Forest Pies / 72
Cod
Chinese-style Glazed Cod / 16
Corn
Authentic Mexican Street Corn / 26
Corned Beef
Corned Beef / 41
Crab Stick
Seasoned Crab Sticks / 19

D,F-H

Dragon Fruit
Dried Dragon Fruit Chips / 61
Duck Leg
Confit Duck Leg with Cranberry Sauce / 53
Fingerling Potato
Rosemary Fingerling Potatoes / 59
Green Olive
Crispy Green Olives / 63
Hake
Breaded Hake and Green Beans Meal / 16
Halibut
Inspired Halibut / 19

K

Kale
Shakshouka with Kale / 28
Spicy Kale Chips / 64
Kiwi
Healthy Kiwi Slices / 60

L

Lamb Chop
Garlicky Lamb Chops / 30

Thyme Lamb Chops / 31
Italian Lamb Chops with Avocado Mayo / 34
Lamb Leg
Cumin Lamb with Red Pepper / 33
Thai Coconut Curry Lamb / 34
Roasted Lamb Leg / 32
Lamb Leg with Brussels Sprouts / 35
Lamb Loin Chop
Lamb Loin Chops with Mushroom Barley / 33
Lamb Rib
Air Fried Lamb Ribs with Mint Yogurt / 31
Lamb Shoulder
Herbed Lamb Shoulder / 30
Lamb Sirloin Steak
Spiced Lamb Steaks and Snap Pea Rice / 36
Lamb Steak
Spiced Lamb Satay / 32
Lamb Tenderloin
Lime Lamb and Chiles / 35

M,O

Milk Chocolate
Tasty Double Chocolate Muffins / 66
Okra
Crunchy Fried Okra / 28
Onion
Classic Onion Rings / 60
Orange Lentil
Ginger Lentil Stew / 24

P

Peach
Peach Brown Betty with Cranberries / 71
Pecan
Candied Eggnog Bread / 70
Pineapple
Simple Pineapple Sticks / 70
Pork
Vietnamese Caramelized Pork with Kimchi / 45
Chinese Eggplant and Pork / 47
Pork Chop
Crusted Pork Chops / 48
Breaded Pork Chops and Cherry Tomato Pasta / 49
Pork Chops and Carrot / 48
Mexican Pork Chops / 47
Pork Loin Chop
Lemony Pork Chop and Leeks / 48
Pork Rib
BBQ Flavored Pork Ribs / 45
Pork Sausage
British Scotch Eggs / 12
Pork Shoulder
Ketchup Pulled Pork / 46
Pork Tenderloin
Pork Medallions / 49
Prawn
Crispy Nacho Prawns / 18

Pumpkin
Greek Pumpkin Bread / 11
Pumpkin Pudding / 72

R

Radish
Herbed Radishes / 25
Red Pepper
Bacon and Spinach Cups / 9
Red Salmon
Homemade Salmon Croquettes / 64
Ribeye Steak
Buttered Ribeye Steak / 39
Roast Beef
Smoked Roast Beef / 40

S

Salmon
Italian Salmon Patties / 19
Salmon, Mushroom and Barley / 20
Cajun Spiced Salmon / 17
Sausage
Bacon Wrapped Sausage / 12
Italian Sausage Meatballs / 46
Scallop
Garlic Lemon Butter Seared Scallops / 21
Buttered Scallops / 18
Shishito Pepper
Shishito Peppers with Dipping Sauce / 23
Shrimp
Spanish Garlic Shrimp / 20
Sirloin Steak
Sirloin Steak with Smashed Yukon Potatoes / 39
Sha Cha Beef with Sugar Snap / 42
Beef and Veggie Kebabs / 40
Skirt Steak
Perfect Skirt Steak / 38
Spinach
Mediterranean Spinach Strata / 14
Squid
Garlic Squid / 17
Strawberry
Tasty Strawberry Slices / 63
Sweet Potato
Sweet Potato Hash / 13

T,W,Z

Tuna
Creamy Penne and Tuna Cakes / 21
Turkey Breast Tenderloin
Spiced Turkey Tenderloin / 56
Walnut
Creamy Chocolate Cake / 68
Walnut Chocolate Brownies / 69
Zucchini
Dill Zucchini Fritters / 11
Vegan Nuggets / 27

Made in the USA
Las Vegas, NV
16 February 2024